Classic
Origami

Classic Origami

P.D. Tuyen

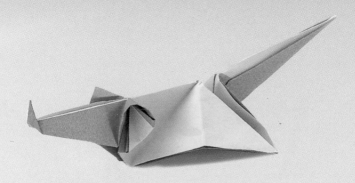

Sterling Publishing Co., Inc.
New York

Contents

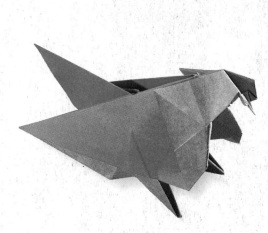

6 8 10 9 7 5

Published 1995 by Sterling Publishing Company, Inc.
387 Park Avenue South, New York, N.Y. 10016
Originally published in Germany by Falken-Verlag GmbH
under the title *Klassisches Origami: Asiatische Faltkinst für Fortgeschrittene*
© 1994 by Falken-Verlag GmbH, Niedernhausen/Ts. Germany
English translation © 1995 by Sterling Publishing Co., Inc.
Distributed in Canada by Sterling Publishing
C/o Canadian Manda Group, One Atlantic Avenue, Suite 105
Toronto, Ontario, Canada M6K 3E7
Distributed in Great Britain and Europe by Cassell PLC
Villiers House, 41/47 Strand, London WC2N 5JE, England
Distributed in Australia by Capricorn Link (Australia) Pty Ltd.
P.O. Box 6651, Baulkham Hills, Business Centre, NSW 2153, Australia
Printed and bound in Hong Kong
All rights reserved

Sterling ISBN 0-8069-1281-2

Library of Congress Cataloging-in-Publication Data

Tuyen, P.D. (Pham Dinh)
[Klassisches Origami. English]
Classic origami / P.D. Tuyen.
p. cm.
Includes index.
ISBN 0-8069-1281-2
1. Origami. I. Title.
TT870.T89 1995
736′.982—dc20
94-42985
CIP

Translated by
Annette Englander

Preface

I grew up in a small town in Vietnam. My childhood was overshadowed by two horrible wars, and toys, as one knows them in many countries, were not available to me. We played with whatever we found out of doors—and with the wonderful animals and flowers made out of paper that my grandfather knew how to fold. One day, when I was about five years old, I asked him whether one could make all of the animals of the world with Origami. Partially amused, partially sad, he admitted that he could only show me how to make some of them; the rest I would have to discover on my own.

Since that time, I have been searching. There is hardly an animal or a flower that I have not tried to fold. I occupied myself with the traditional folding techniques, and I went down new paths. Due to my profession as an architect, I have much to do with three-dimensional plans, with drawings, with beauty. It is likely because of that I began to design my own folding models as well. In this book you will find twenty-six of them.

Origami, from the Japanese *ori* (to fold) and *gami* (paper), is to me the art of paper folding as it is practised everywhere in Japan, China, and South and Southeast Asia, and which follows these strict basic rules: the starting material for each figure is a square piece of paper. Helping devices of any kind are taboo, and that includes scissors and glue. What counts is the skilled hand of the artist alone.

How does one judge a new Origami figure? First, by how the original and the Origami figure correspond in shape and proportion, and second, by the number and distinctness of the folding steps necessary to achieve the figure.

The world of Origami is rich in variety and surprises. No matter how practised one might be at folding, there will always be a figure at which one at first fails. My wish is that you derive the same pleasure out of such challenges as I do, whether you want only to make Origami toys, or whether you fold because if furthers your concentration and brings you closer to a state of inner peace.

Yours,
Pham Dinh Tuyen

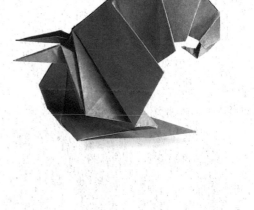

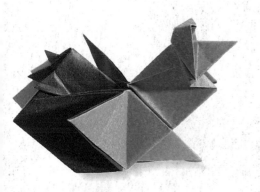

Origami, Yesterday and Today

There are differing opinions and interpretations of Origami's long history, but all agree that it was the Chinese who invented the paper and began what is now known as the art of paper folding. Origami probably served from the beginning as an integral part of religious ceremonies. although when this was, no one knows for certain. In past decades, however, Origami experienced a renaissance—especially in Japan, where one folds today according to the classic rules. Paper folding also came into fashion in Europe and the United States, but it is not the classic form. There, scissors and glue may be used to complete paper-folding works.

By incorporating such technology, almost everything can be modelled: people, plants, animals, houses, even bicycles and cars of all kinds.

Sacral Art

In East-Asian countries, like China or Vietnam, the deceased are traditionally buried with a number of items of household goods because it is believed that the dead need these things in the world on the other side. One of the duties of surviving family members is a yearly sacrificial service, at the anniversary of the death of a relative. After the service, in contrast to the funeral, smaller paper models of useful articles and animals are given to the sacrificial fire. These are intended to ease the existence of the deceased in the other world and, in turn, may induce the departed member to oversee and protect the safety, health, and wealth of the living relative. Deceased family members are not the only ones to be enticed into a favorable mood with sacrifices. At religious holidays, sacrifices are also given to various ghosts. Of course, the bigger or more magnificent the sacrificed object, the more certain one is to obtain the help of those in the other world. The construction of these grander offerings has always been done by special tradespeople. A skeleton is first built out of wood or bamboo, then covered with paper or fabric. In the case of smaller objects, a skeleton is not needed, especially when the figure consists only of paper. Some of the larger paper models can only be created through cutting and gluing; other figures can be easily folded. These include, among others, small boxes or little animals. It is likely that the people learned more and more to make these simple folded objects themselves, to contribute to the decoration of the graves of loved ones, either out of piety or because of the low cost. This we see as the beginning of the popularizing of Origami.

Folk Art

At one point, people must have discovered the gracefulness and the strange beauty of the Origami figures and turned to constructing them as an end in itself. Paper folding became an art form to be practised in everyday life when cheap paper became available. Of course, besides classic Origami, creation techniques that included the use of scissors and glue in working the paper into a figure became widespread.

The path throughout many centuries to a higher level of folding was quite burdensome for the followers of Origami. In the art of paper folding, it is not sufficient to simply transfer the form of the original onto the copy, as is done, for example, by a carver. One has to be able to imagine, before, the inner structure of the folds that finally leads to the outer form—which must also be in accordance with the original. For this, one needs a good measure of three-dimensional imagination and an exact knowledge of the possible basic forms. In addition, the sequence of the individual folding steps is important. A tiny mistake leads with certainty to a wrong result.

If all these small figures could have been preserved over the centuries, then Origami would have been perfected early on in the history of civilization. But there were only a few books and very little knowledge of geometrical form. Origami teachers introduced and passed down the art of folding paper step by step. This was the popular way to convey knowledge, but who can memorize the many steps needed for the construction of a complicated figure? In addition, the fact is that paper figures do not last for an especially long time. If a pattern was lost, there was hardly a chance to repeat the artwork. It is therefore understandable that, despite a tradition that spans centuries, only a few patterns were handed down from long ago. (Three of them, the Sitting Crane, the Hat of a Ghost with the Name Mr. Cong, and the Boat with Two Roofs, are illustrated on these pages for you.) They are mostly figures that are completed in six to ten folding steps—a number of steps easy enough to remember.

In Japan, Origami came back into favor after the Second World War. The symbol of this development, the Sitting Crane, is among the handed-down patterns, maybe the most beautiful one. It represents one's longing for life and peace. The Sitting Crane became world famous through a young Japanese woman. Suffering from cancer caused by an atom bomb blast over Japan, she folded one thousand cranes in the hope of becoming healthy again through the force of the life symbol.

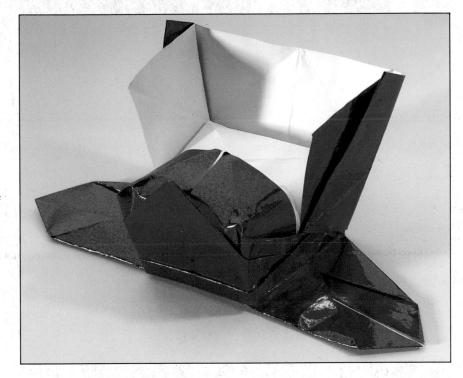

New Trends

What does one need in order to fold Origami figures successfully? The most important thing is to take pleasure in creating; in addition, as we said, a three-dimensional imagination, and a basic knowledge of geometry. The inventors of Origami figures today write down all the folding steps using a geometrical symbol-language. Its use contributes much to the spread of the art of paper folding because it provides an essential and clean means of communication between Origami teachers and students, between authors and readers. This is the system used in this book.

Today, there are three lines of development in the art of paper folding. The first, the classic school, strictly adheres to tradition—the starting form is a square and no cutting or gluing is permitted. Variations are created solely through the type and/or color of the paper used. The second, so-called reformed, trend allows rectangles and triangles also as starting forms. The third school tolerates cutting and gluing, and permits the assembling of figures to make new forms.

In this book, we adhere strictly to the rules of the first line of development—the classic, traditional school. Although we could, of course, model the legs of our Spider much more easily using the scissors, it is exactly that, the overcoming of the difficulties caused by the rules, which is the charm of Origami. Yet, as you can see, with some practice it is still possible to create models in keeping with the original, because Origami is simply ingenious in its diversity.

Before the Folding Starts

Choosing the Paper

Besides a sound, much-practised folding technique, it is the paper that is all-important to the ancient art of paper folding. Beautiful, graceful Origami figures can be folded out of all sorts of paper, so long as it is soft enough to be easily bent but stiff enough to give the figures the sturdiness to stand upright. (A tip: typing paper is just right for the Origami beginner.)

At first, use a larger-format paper; for example, 8½ × 8½ inches (21 cm × 21 cm), but always use a square piece. Take into consideration, when you purchase the paper, that its quality and the color contribute much to the beauty of the figures.

Folding Correctly

Is this your first encounter with Origami? Then you could find our animal figures complicated. Be brave, though, and have patience. At the beginning, it can easily take you an hour to complete a figure, following the text and illustrations. Keep to the basic rules, even when it becomes difficult! After each folding step, compare your work with the pattern shown, and only take the next step when you are sure of your ground.

We have divided complicated folds into in-between steps to make things easier. Your fold creases should be straight and sharp, and should correspond exactly to the pattern. Concentrate! In the art of Origami, constant practice alone makes perfect. Little by little, you will see, your figures will acquire the precision and grace of Origami.

Symbols

The instructions to work each fold step by step are provided in the drawings, as symbols, as well as in the text. It will help to memorize these symbols, beginning with those for the important mountain and valley folds. Although no absolutely binding symbol system exists at the present time, the symbols used here are found most often in Origami texts, and we believe they will eventually assert themselves and become the standard.

Instruction	Symbol	Result

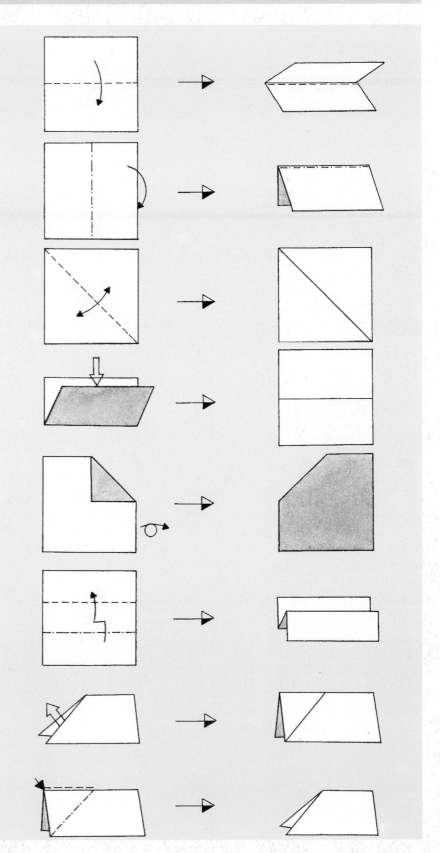

1. Valley fold (a series of short dashes): A fold inward.

2. Mountain fold (dash-dot-dash series): A fold outward.

3. Prefold (two-headed arrow): Crease to fold both inward and outward.

4. Open (outlined arrow towards fold): Opened-up fold.

5. Turn over (arrow with loop): Figure turned around.

6. Zigzag (zigzag arrow): Paper folded in accordion pleats.

7. Pull out (outlined arrow): Section pulled outward.

8. Combination fold: Consecutive mountain and valley folds (see page 10).

Combination Folds

We call several mountain and valley folds, executed consecutively, a combination fold. There are numerous variations, so make sure, before you work the fold, exactly where the mountain and/or valley folds are to be made. The symbols in the drawings, as presented and explained on page 9, will help you. Always prefold along the drawn-in lines. Following are some examples of combination folds for practice. These will make the construction of our Origami figures easier for you. It will not hurt to do the same folds several times in a row.

Instructions and Folding Steps

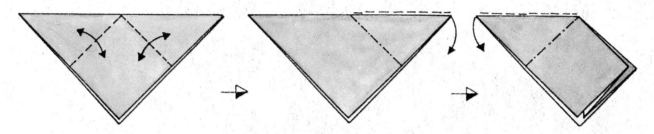

Prefold. Bend the right corner inward with valley and mountain folds; do the same on the left.

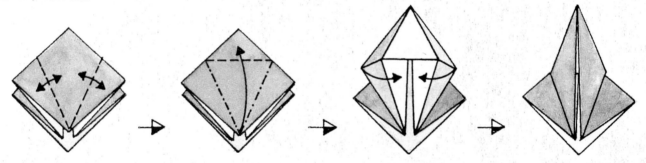

Prefold. Pull the lower point of the square upwards (with two mountain folds and the valley fold). Fold and flatten the two corners onto the middle line.

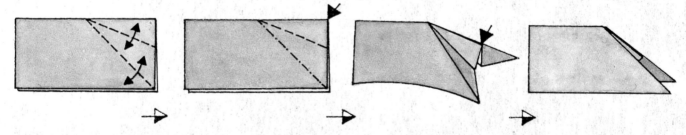

Prefold. Push the right corner inward with valley and mountain folds.

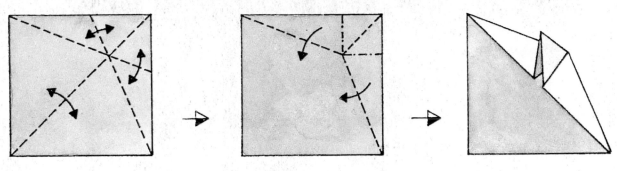

Prefold. With three valley and two
mountain folds, bend the corner onto
the middle line so that it stands
vertically upwards.

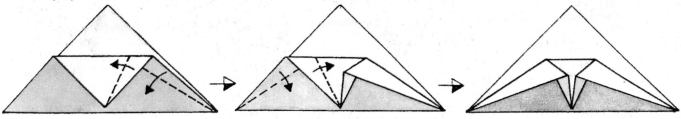

Bend the right corner with two valley
folds; the same for the left corner.

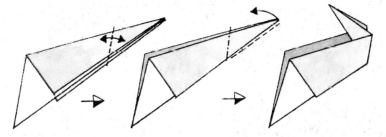

Prefold. Turn the point inward with valley and mountain folds.

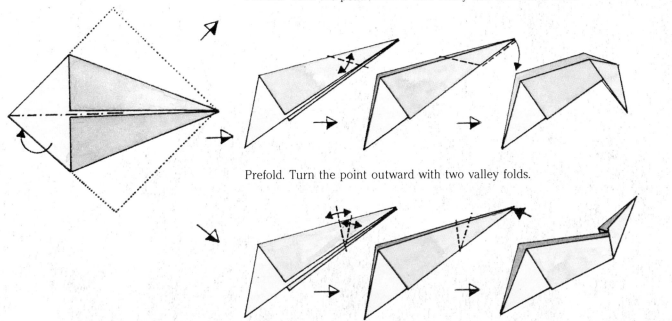

Prefold. Turn the point outward with two valley folds.

Prefold. With valley and mountain folds, press the point upwards and to the left.

11

Basic Form I

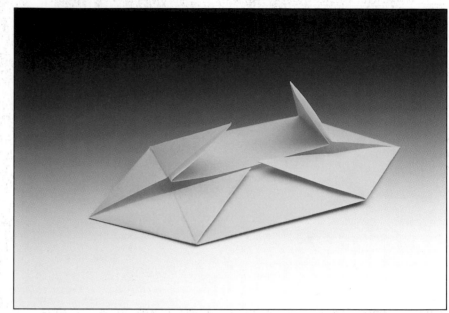

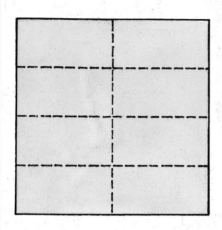

1. Prefold a square piece of paper along the markings.

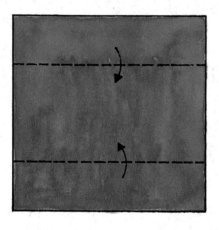

2. Fold the two outer sections inward with valley folds.

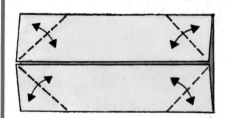

3. Prefold at all corners.

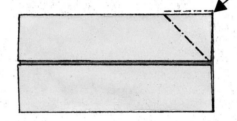

4. Combination fold one corner, . . .

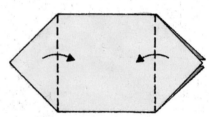

5. . . . then the other corners.

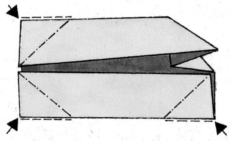

6. Turn over the form.

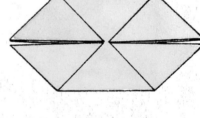

7. Fold the two front points inward with valley folds.

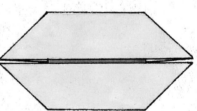

8. Completed Basic Form I.

Dragonfly

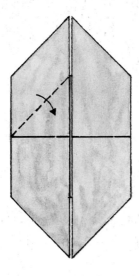

1. Starting point is Basic Form I. Valley fold one side in to the middle line.

2. Valley fold the central edge outward.

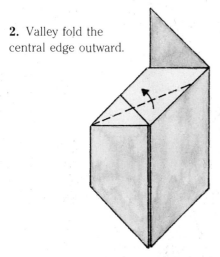

3. Valley fold the inner tip outward.

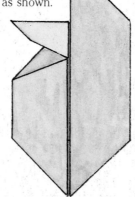

4. Fold the remaining three corners as shown.

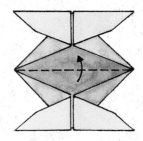

5. Valley fold the lower part upwards.

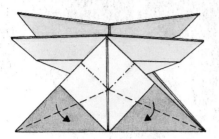

6. Fold front part with a combination fold . . .

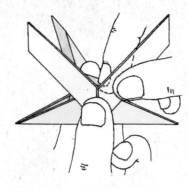

10. . . . upwards, pressing them to the body; repeat on the reverse.

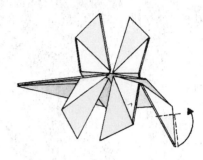

13. . . . then combination fold upwards, . . .

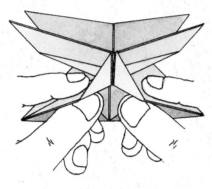

7. . . . outward and down.

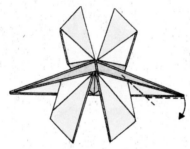

11. Valley fold all wings downwards.

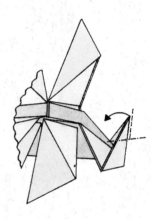

14. . . . and then inward; the head is finished.

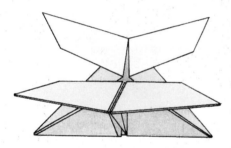

8. Repeat the combination fold on the reverse. Front view shown.

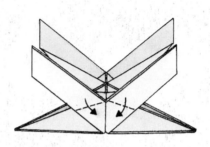

12. Combination fold one point downwards, . . .

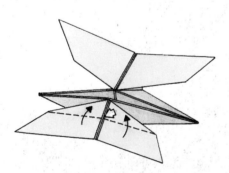

9. Place your finger at the middle fold, as shown, and combination fold the wings . . .

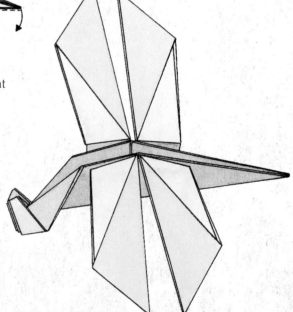

15. Completed dragonfly.

Squirrel

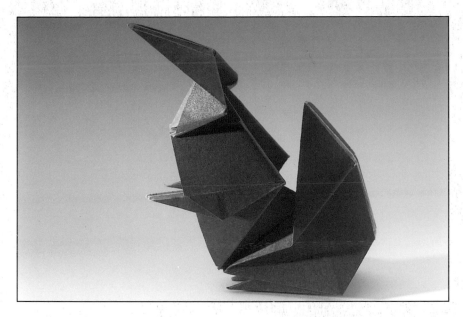

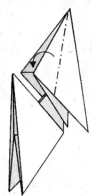

7. Mountain fold the edge (top left) on each side inward.

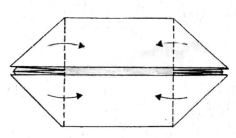

1. Starting point is step 6 of Basic Form I. Fold the four front points inward with valley folds.

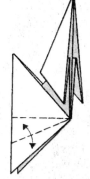

4. Mountain fold the upper back section rearwards and down.

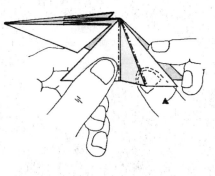

8. Combination fold the rear paws . . .

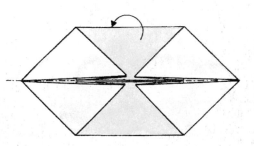

2. Mountain fold in the middle.

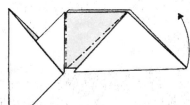

5. Combination fold the right point . . .

9. . . . as shown in the drawing.

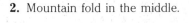

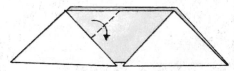

3. Valley fold the upper front section where marked.

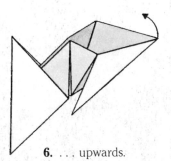

6. . . . upwards.

10. Combination fold the point of one rear paw . . .

11. . . . upwards.

12. Repeat the fold on the other side.

13. Combination fold the front paws upwards.

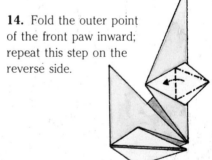

14. Fold the outer point of the front paw inward; repeat this step on the reverse side.

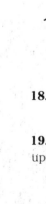

15. Fold the tips of both front paws outward again; valley fold the top sections of both rear paws downwards.

16. Fold upper sections of both front paws downwards. Bend the points of both rear paws slightly . . .

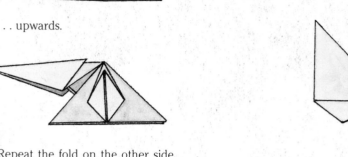

17. . . . downwards. With combination fold, press the upper and lower middle edges . . .

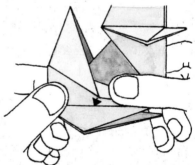

18. . . . downwards, for the tail.

19. Combination fold the upper corner . . .

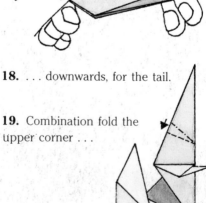

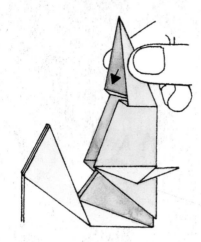

20. . . . as shown.

21. Combination fold the point to make ears.

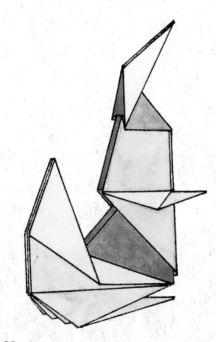

22. Completed squirrel.

Basic Form II

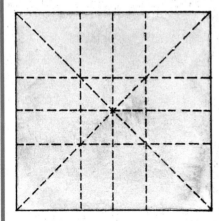

1. Divide a square piece of paper into sections by prefolding at the marked lines.

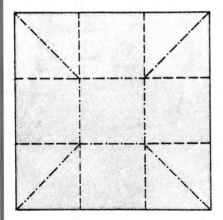

2. Combination fold as marked.

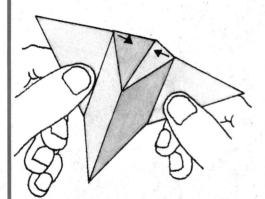

3. Valley fold at the center line . . .

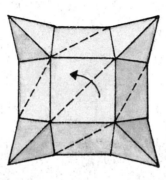

4. . . . and as shown.

5. Completed Basic Form II.

Turtle

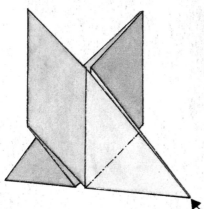

1. Starting point is Basic Form II. Mountain fold at the marked line, . . .

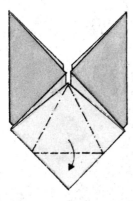

2. . . . then press the right lower corner up into the middle.

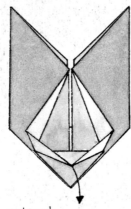

4. . . . outward.

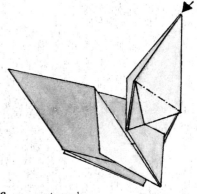

6. . . . outward and push the outer point inward.

3. Repeat steps 1 and 2 on the reverse. Combination fold; do not forget to prefold. Now, pull the upper corner of the square . . .

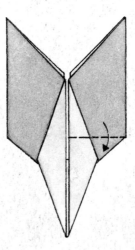

5. With a valley fold, bend the right section . . .

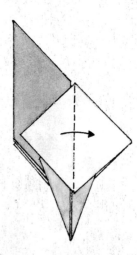

7. Fold the left corner of the square created by the last step . . .

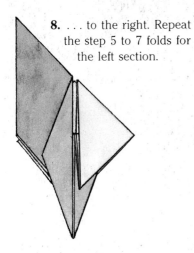

8. . . . to the right. Repeat the step 5 to 7 folds for the left section.

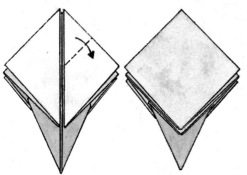

9. Bend the upper point diagonally to upright, . . .

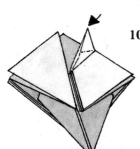

10. . . . and press outer edges downwards.

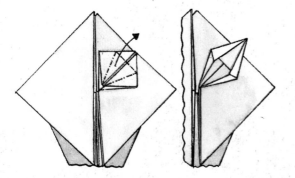

11. Combination fold.

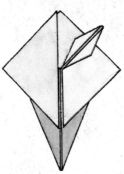

12. Do the same steps also at the left and two lower corners.

13. Turn all created feet . . .

14. . . . inward.

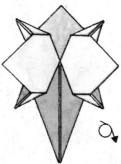

15. Turn over the form.

16. Fold both lower corners upwards.

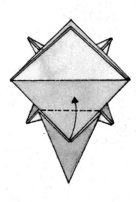

17. Valley fold upwards.

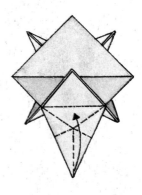

18. Combination fold.

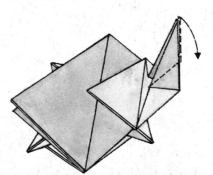

19. Bend the point downwards, following the valley-fold lines.

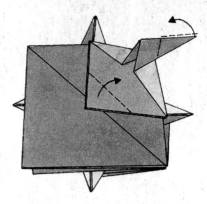

20. Bend the point upwards at the valley-fold lines, and valley fold the left corner marked to the right.

21. Bend the point of the head inward. Valley fold the turtle's shell forward as marked.

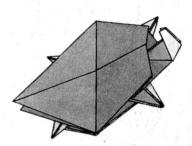

22. Turn over the form.

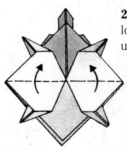

23. Fold the lower sections upwards.

24. Valley fold upwards along the marked line.

25. Valley fold downwards.

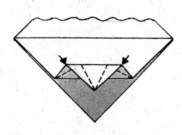

26. Make the tail with a combination fold.

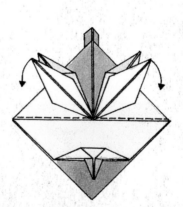

27. Fold the feet downwards again.

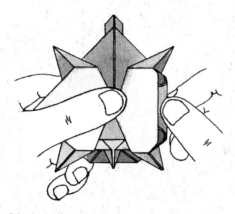

28. Mountain fold all five corners as marked . . .

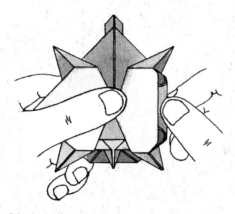

29. . . . in to the form.

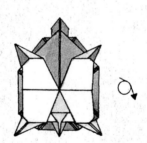

30. Turn over the form.

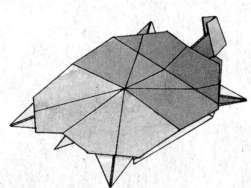

31. Completed turtle. Making more creases on the shell will make it look nicer.

Crane

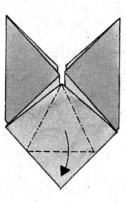

1. Starting point is step 3 of the Turtle, based on Basic Form II. Combination fold, . . .

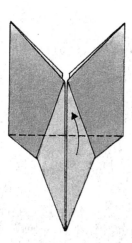

2. . . . then pull the upper corner of the square forward.

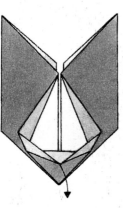

3. Repeat step 1 and 2 folds on the reverse; bend the wing upwards where marked.

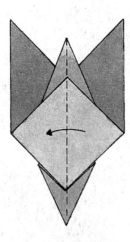

4. Valley fold the entire form at the middle.

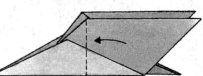

5. Bend the front wing vertically upwards . . .

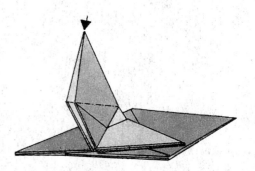

6. . . . and press the outer tip of the wing inward.

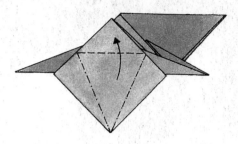

7. Combination fold . . .

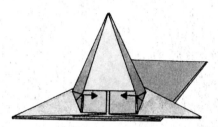

8. . . . upwards.

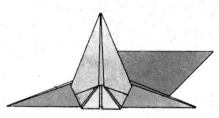

9. Repeat all step 5 to 8 folds on the reverse.

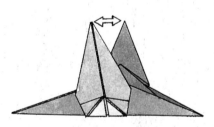

10. Open up the figure.

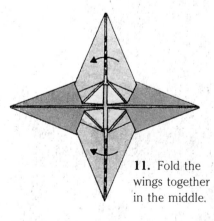

11. Fold the wings together in the middle.

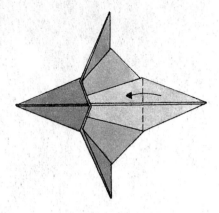

12. Fold the right wing to the left.

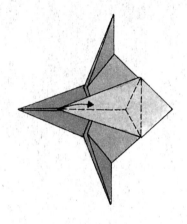

13. Combination fold so that the point extends upwards.

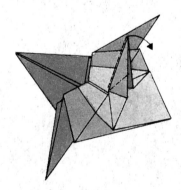

14. Fold the point inward with a combination fold.

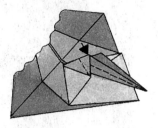

15. Combination fold . . .

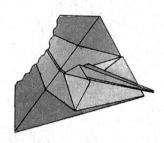

16. . . . to make the feet smaller.

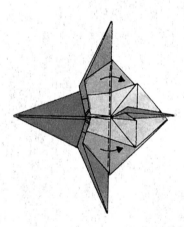

17. Open up the wings in the middle again.

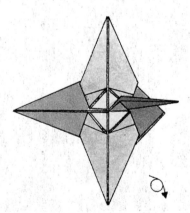

18. Turn over the form.

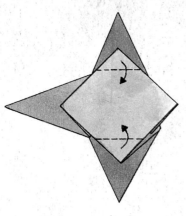

19. Fold the corners in to the middle.

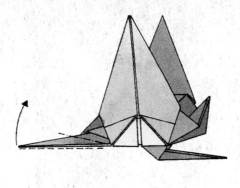

22. Bend the neck diagonally upwards with a combination fold.

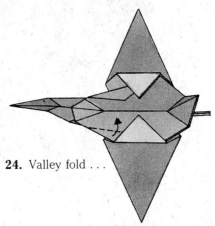

24. Valley fold . . .

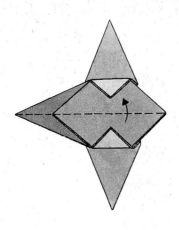

20. Valley fold the form in the middle.

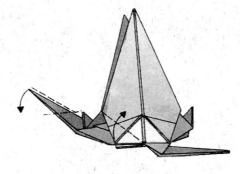

23. Fold the corner as marked on both sides; combination fold the beak.

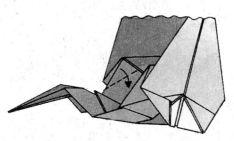

25. . . . at the places marked.

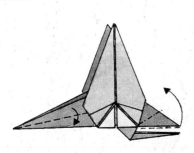

21. Combination fold the right corner inward, and fold the left point, respectively, into halves.

26. Completed crane.

Basic Form III

5. . . . and pull the lower corner of the square upwards.

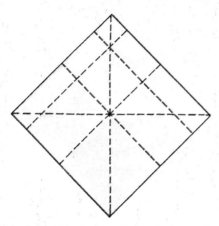

1. Prefold a square piece of paper at the marked lines.

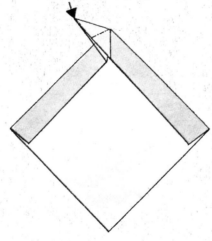

3. . . . so that the corner remains standing up; press the outer edge of the corner downwards.

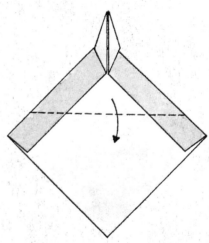

6. Valley fold downwards (where prefold lines cross).

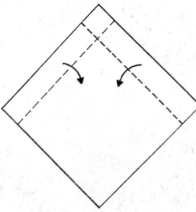

2. With the white side upwards, valley fold at the lines . . .

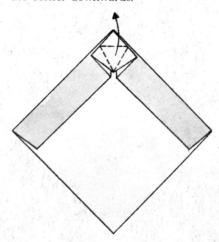

4. Combination fold, . . .

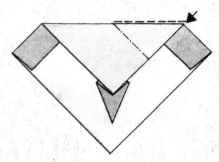

7. Combination fold; this moves the arrow-marked corner inward onto the diagonal.

8. Repeat these folds . . .

9. . . . on the left side.

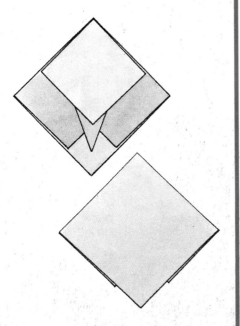

10. Completed Basic Form III

Peacock

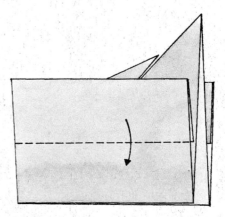

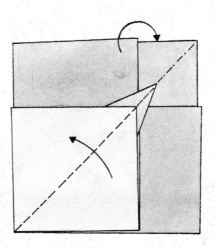

1. Starting point is Basic Form III. Fold the smaller square upwards and the rear square downwards.

2. On both sides, valley fold downwards, . . .

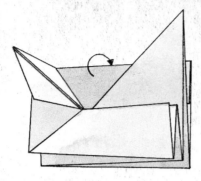

3. . . . while holding the figure at the bottom right, and fold in the left rear corner.

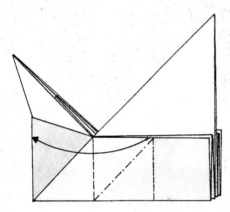

4. Pull the section marked forward, in the direction of the arrow . . .

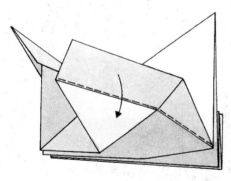

5. . . . and fold the edge under as shown.

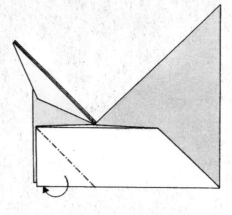

6. Repeat steps 4 and 5 on the reverse; bend the corners on both sides inward.

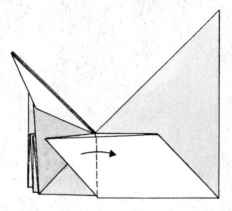

7. Valley fold the points on both sides to the right.

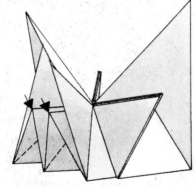

8. Combination fold the corners inward as shown.

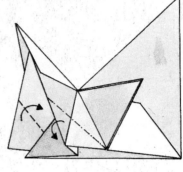

9. Fold the two corners diagonally inward.

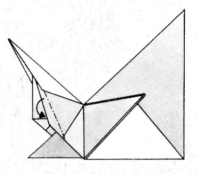

10. Fold the edges on each side inward as shown.

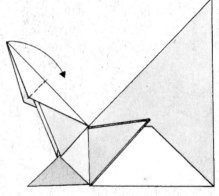

11. Valley fold the upper point downwards.

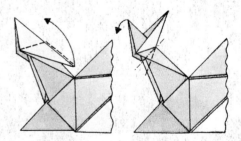

12. Combination fold upwards. Then press downwards as marked for a combination fold that forms the head.

26

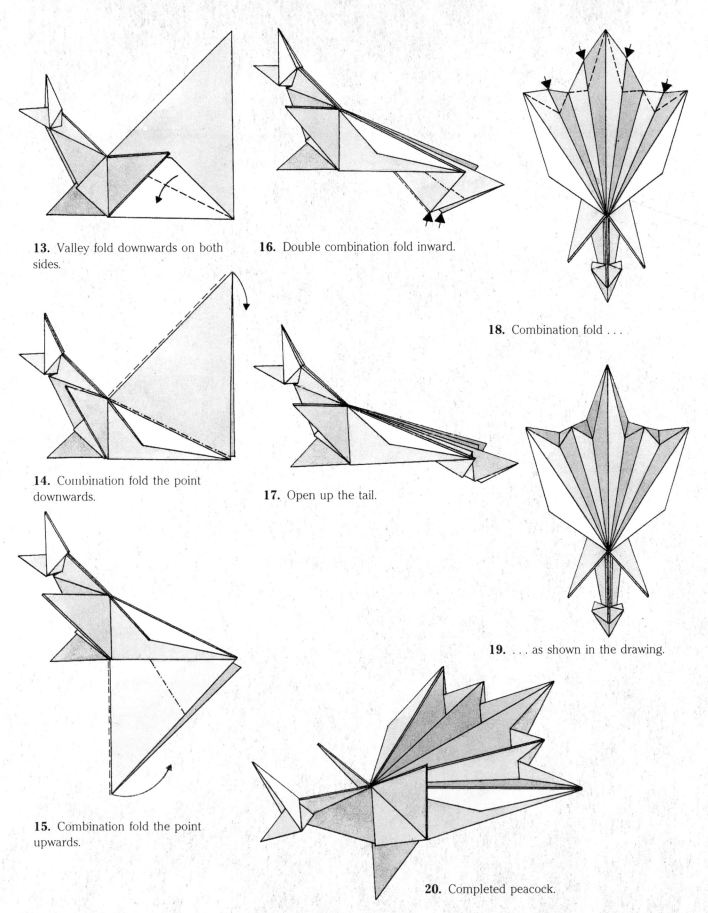

13. Valley fold downwards on both sides.

14. Combination fold the point downwards.

15. Combination fold the point upwards.

16. Double combination fold inward.

17. Open up the tail.

18. Combination fold . . .

19. . . . as shown in the drawing.

20. Completed peacock.

Rooter

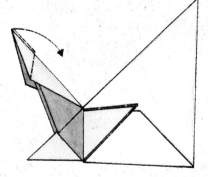

1. Starting point is step 11 of the Peacock, based on Basic Form III. Combination fold at the point.

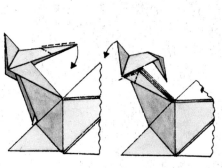

2. Combination fold again to bend the point downwards; then press down on the head.

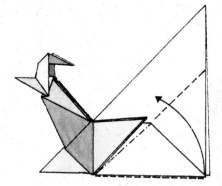

3. Pull the right lower corner upwards and to the inside.

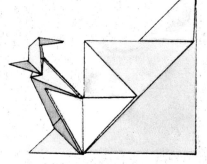

4. Repeat the step on the reverse.

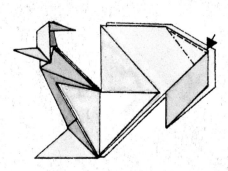

6. With a combination fold, press the marked corner inward.

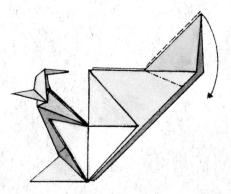

5. Fold the tail inward and down.

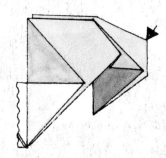

7. Repeat the step on the reverse.

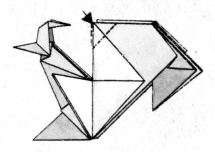

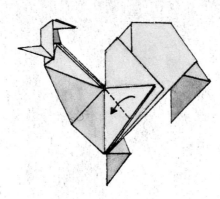

8. Combination fold the corner inward.

12. Fold it downwards as marked.

14. Repeat steps 11 to 13 on the reverse.

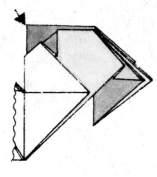

9. Repeat the step on the reverse.

13. Push the upper tip of the wing inward.

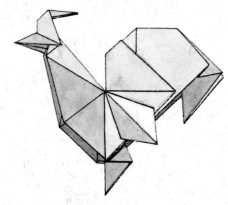

15. Completed rooster.

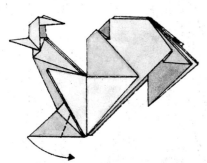

10. Pull the foot to vertical, towards the right.

11. Valley fold the wing to the right.

Hen

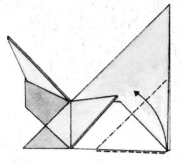

1. Starting point is step 11 of the Peacock, based on Basic Form III. Fold the corner up and inward.

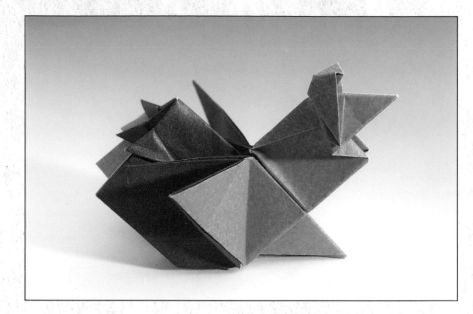

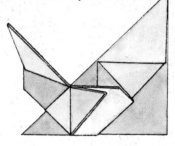

2. Repeat the step on the reverse.

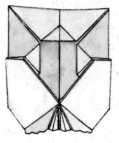

5. Fold form back together.

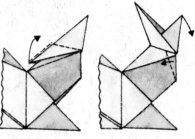

8. Fold the tip upwards, then push the head down, making a combination fold.

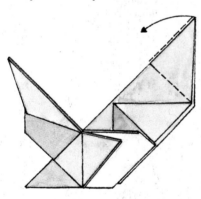

3. Fold the right upper corner downwards, opening the form in the middle.

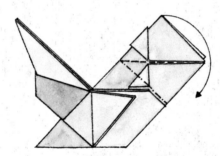

6. Combination fold the corner inward along the lines.

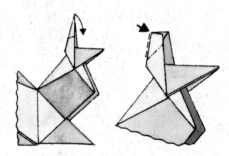

9. Form the crest as shown.

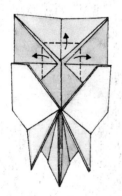

4. Valley fold the corners.

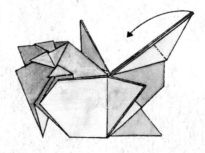

7. Turn over the form. Fold the point to the left.

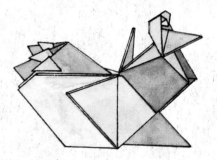

10. Completed hen.

Basic Form IV

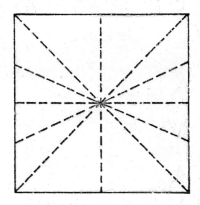

1. Prefold a square piece of paper at the marked lines.

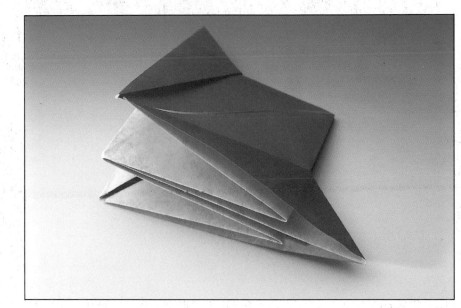

2. With the white side upwards, mountain fold.

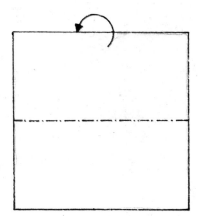

3. Push the right corner inward with a combination fold.

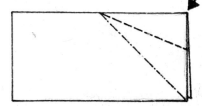

4. Repeat the step on the left side.

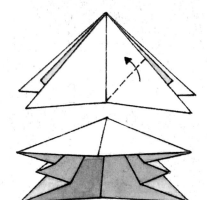

5. Bend the front right corner . . .

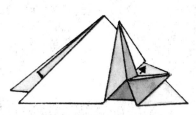

6. . . . upwards.

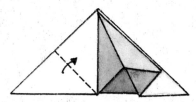

7. Repeat the step on the left side.

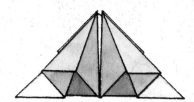

8. Repeat steps 5 to 7 on the reverse.

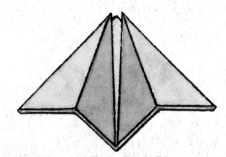

9. Completed Basic Form IV.

Hare

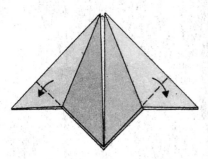

1. Starting point is Basic Form IV. Unfold the surfaces.

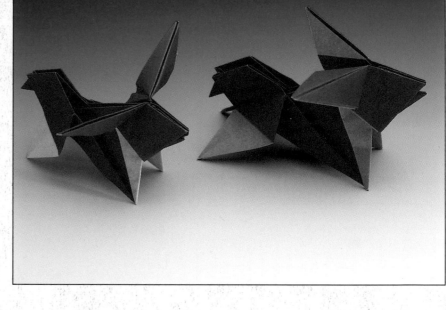

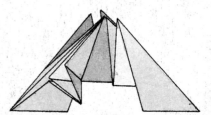

2. Raise the lower edge of the paper . . .

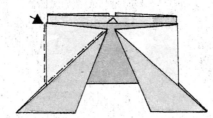

5. Combination fold inward.

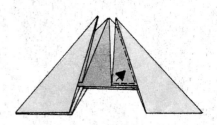

8. . . . and fold the section inward.

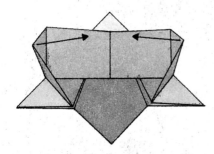

3. . . . and fold the sides inward.

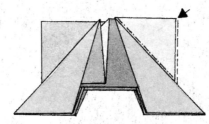

6. Repeat the step on the other side.

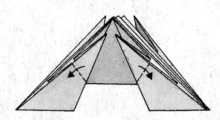

9. Repeat the step at the three remaining corners.

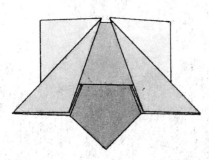

4. Repeat steps 1 to 3 on the reverse.

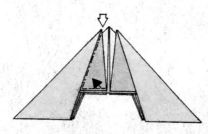

7. Repeat steps 5 and 6 on the reverse; pull the upper point outward, . . .

10. Valley fold all four points downwards.

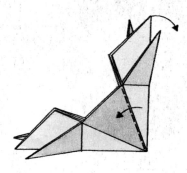

11. Valley fold top section to the left, . . .

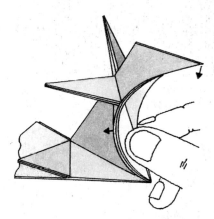

12. . . . and valley fold also on the reverse, so head is pressed downwards.

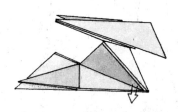

13. Pull the right lower point outward as shown, on both sides.

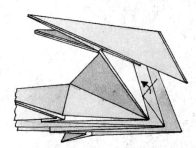

14. Fold the middle section to one side.

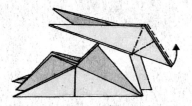

15. Form the head by combination folding . . .

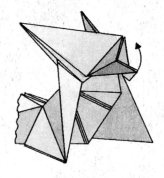

16. . . . inward.

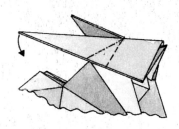

17. Fold both ears forward.

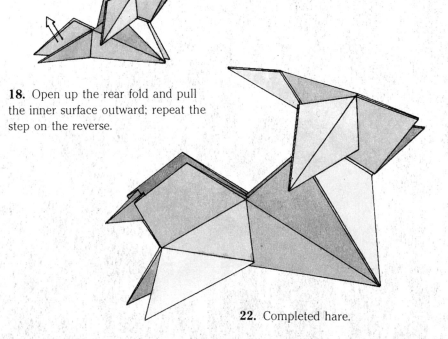

18. Open up the rear fold and pull the inner surface outward; repeat the step on the reverse.

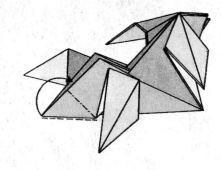

19. Fold the tail section with a combination fold.

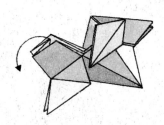

20. Valley fold both legs downwards.

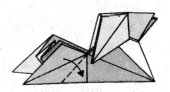

21. Form the tail.

22. Completed hare.

Marten

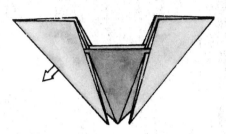

1. Starting point is step 10 of the Hare, based on Basic Form IV. Open up the entire left side.

2. Press the two upper edges to the inside.

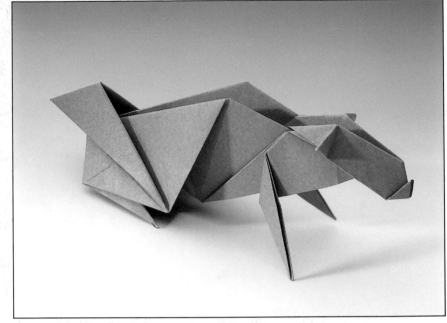

4. . . . and mountain fold on the reverse side.

6. Combination fold, . . .

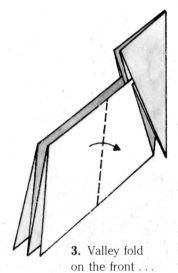

3. Valley fold on the front . . .

5. Lift the point and press it down at the mid-line of the triangle.

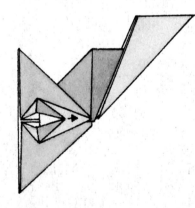

7. . . . then lift the left point and pull it to the right.

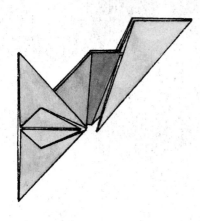

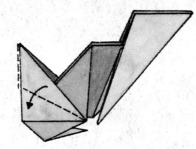

11. Combination fold down and outward.

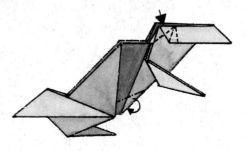

13. Mountain fold on both sides of the abdomen; also form the ears.

8. Repeat steps 6 and 7 on the reverse.

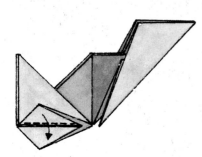

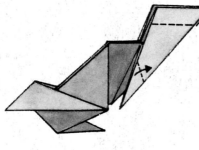

12. Bend the front legs forward, and bend the head folds to the outside.

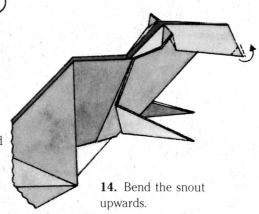

9. Valley fold downwards on both sides

14. Bend the snout upwards.

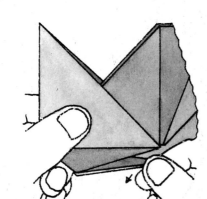

15. Completed marten.

10. Pull the point downwards slightly and press to form feet.

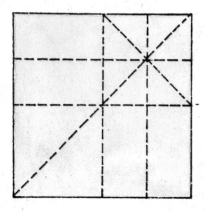

1. Prefold a square piece of paper at the marked lines.

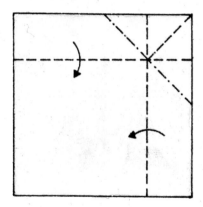

2. With the white side upward, fold as marked . . .

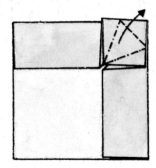

4. Combination fold; . . .

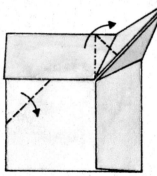

6. At the top arrow, pull the paper upwards in the direction shown, . . .

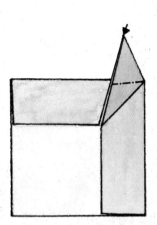

3. . . . so the corner stands vertically upwards. Press the corner tip downwards.

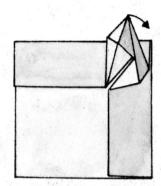

5. . . . then pull the corner of the square upwards and press.

7. . . . and fold it to the right.

8. Fold the corner upwards.

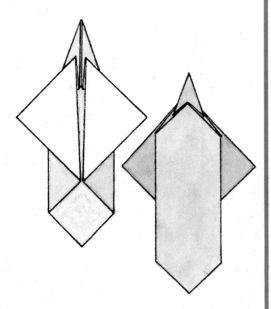

9. Repeat steps 6 to 8 on the other side.

10. Completed Basic Form V

Elephant

3. Turn the form. Open the lower section . . .

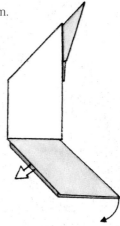

1. Starting point is Basic Form V. Mountain fold the figure at the middle line.

2. Combination fold inward.

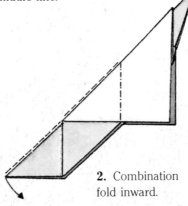

4. . . . and fold it upwards as marked, . . .

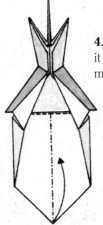

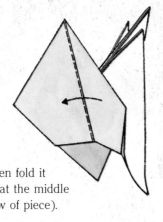

5. . . . then fold it together at the middle (rear view of piece).

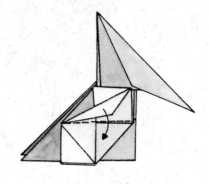

9. . . . downwards.

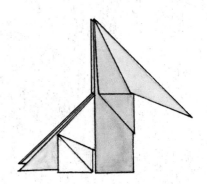

13. Valley fold downwards.

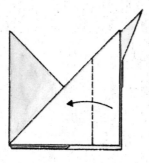

6. The head is made up of two symmetrical parts. First, valley fold the left section as shown.

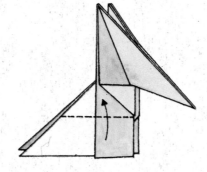

10. Lift the right lower corner upwards . . .

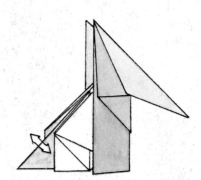

14. Repeat steps 10 to 13 on the reverse.

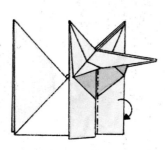

7. Repeat the step on the other side. This pulls the head downwards.

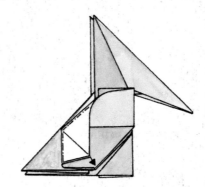

11. . . . and press the left corner to the right.

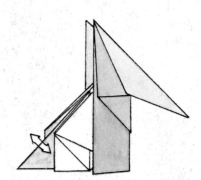

15. Open up the left fold (rear body region), . . .

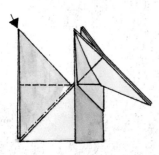

8. Push in the point (marked with arrow) and combination fold . . .

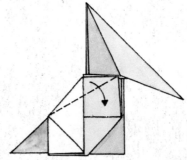

12. Valley fold downwards.

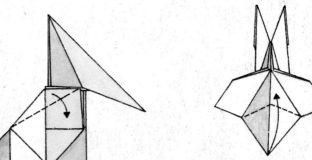

16. . . . fold the lower corner upwards . . .

17. . . . and downwards again as marked.

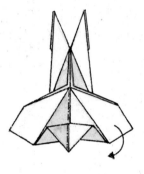

18. Mountain fold figure together.

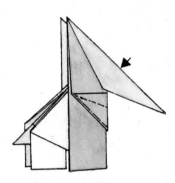

19. Push down on the head, and combination fold . . .

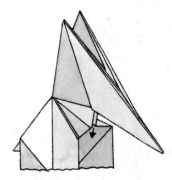

20. . . . to the inside and downwards.

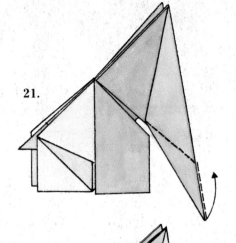

21.

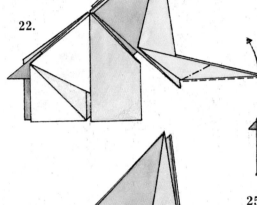

22.

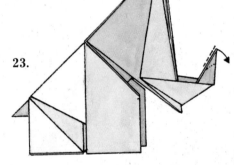

23.

21 to 23. Form the trunk, as shown in the drawings.

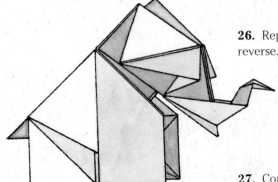

24. Form the ear with a combination fold . . .

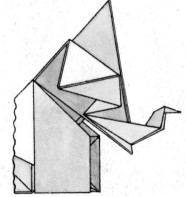

25. . . . and press downwards.

26. Repeat steps 24 and 25 on the reverse.

27. Completed elephant.

Mouse

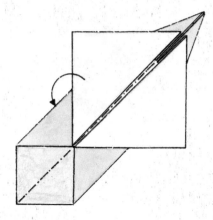

1. Starting point is Basic Form V. Fold figure together at the middle line.

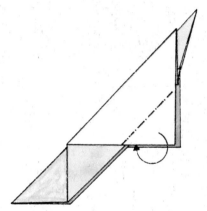

2. Mountain fold corners inward on both sides.

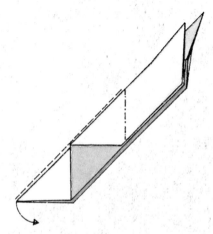

3. Combination fold inward.

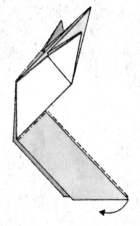

4. Combination fold to the inside and upwards.

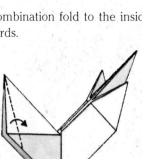

5. Valley fold on both sides.

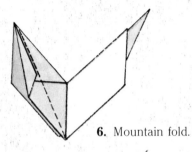

6. Mountain fold.

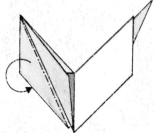

7. Valley fold to the back.

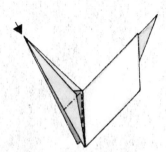

8. Push down on the tail to combination fold it . . .

40

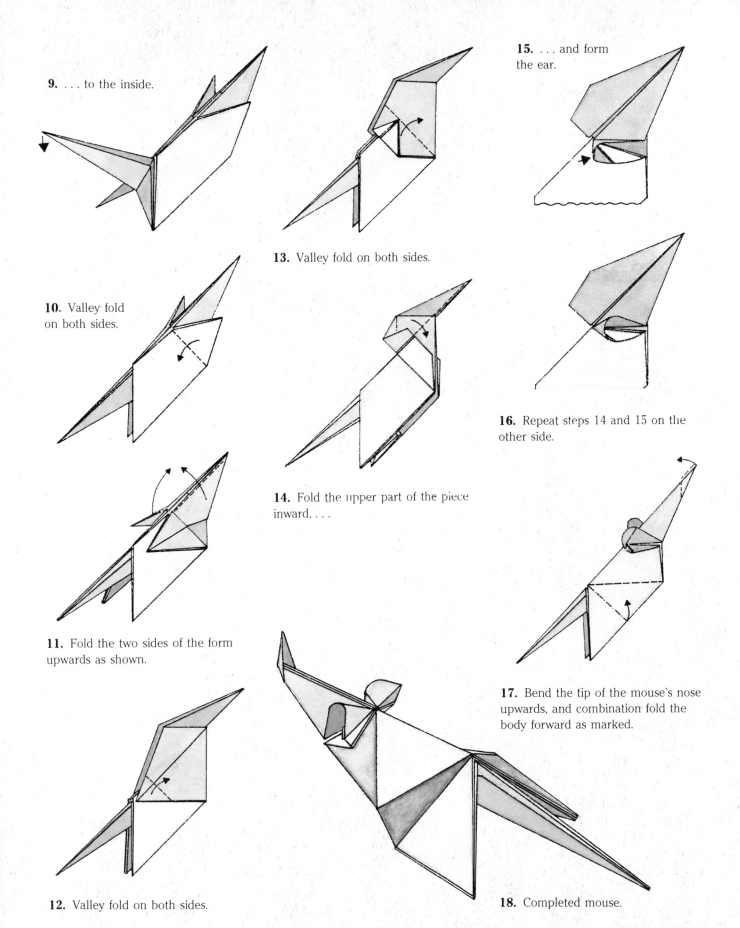

9. . . . to the inside.

10. Valley fold on both sides.

11. Fold the two sides of the form upwards as shown.

12. Valley fold on both sides.

13. Valley fold on both sides.

14. Fold the upper part of the piece inward, . . .

15. . . . and form the ear.

16. Repeat steps 14 and 15 on the other side.

17. Bend the tip of the mouse's nose upwards, and combination fold the body forward as marked.

18. Completed mouse.

Fox

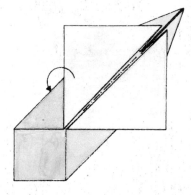

1. Starting point is Basic Form V. Mountain fold the form together at the middle.

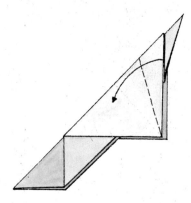

2. Valley fold in the direction of the arrow.

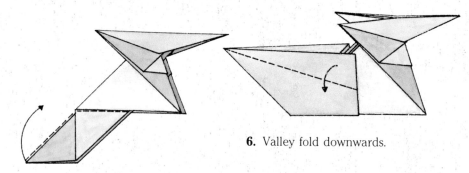

4. Bend the tail upwards on the outside.

6. Valley fold downwards.

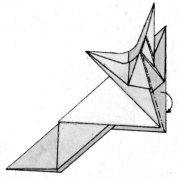

3. Repeat the step on the other side.

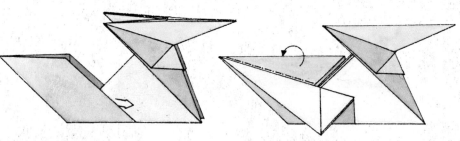

5. On both sides, pull out the paper flaps that lie on the inside.

7. Repeat the step on the reverse.

42

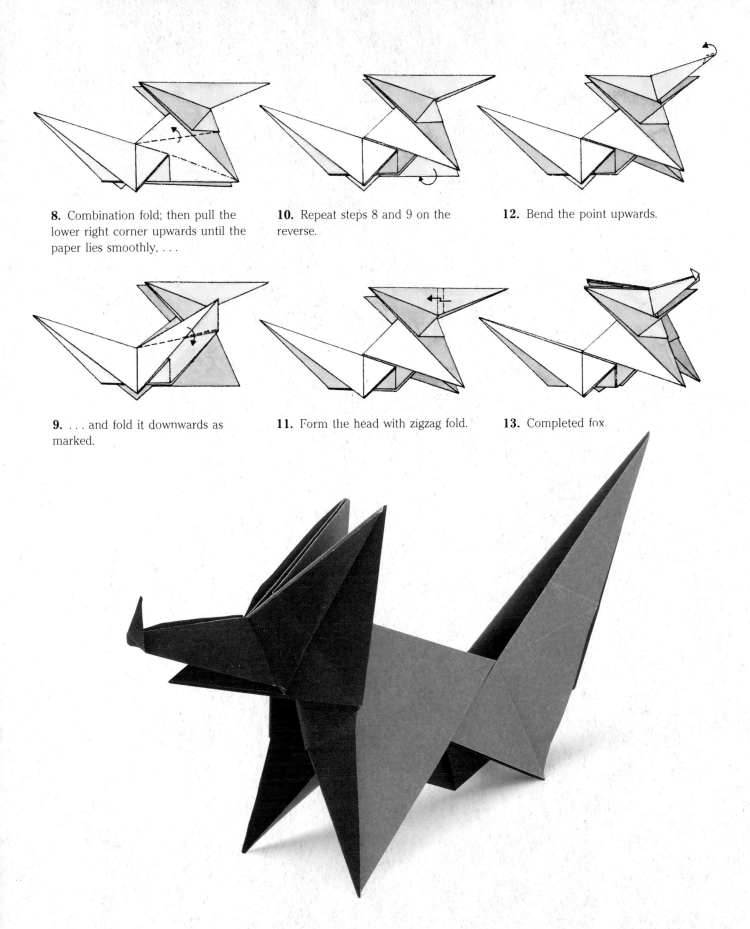

8. Combination fold; then pull the lower right corner upwards until the paper lies smoothly, . . .

10. Repeat steps 8 and 9 on the reverse.

12. Bend the point upwards.

9. . . . and fold it downwards as marked.

11. Form the head with zigzag fold.

13. Completed fox.

Basic Form VI

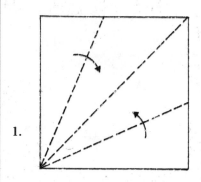

1.

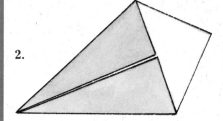

2.

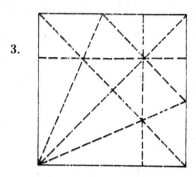

3.

1 to 3. Prefold a square piece of paper as marked; with the white side of the Origami paper facing upwards.

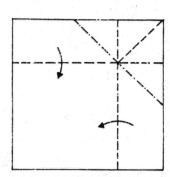

4. Fold at the marked lines, . . .

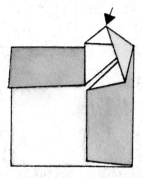

5. . . . so the corner stands vertically upwards; then press the outer edges downwards.

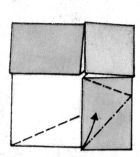

6. Pull the lower corner marked . . .

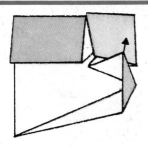

7. . . . upwards, using a combination fold.

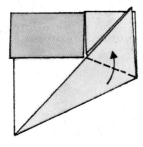

8. Press the section flat.

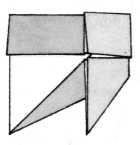

9. Repeat steps 6 to 8 on the other side.

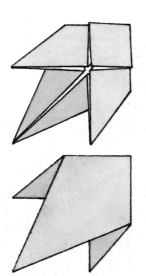

10. Completed Basic Form VI.

Snail

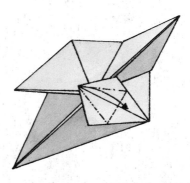

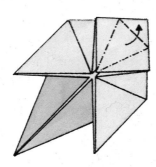

1. Starting point is Basic Form VI. Combination fold, . . .

3. Position the wing upwards, across the middle, and press the edges flat.

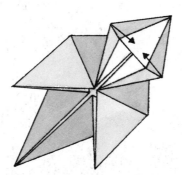

2. . . . pullling the corner outward.

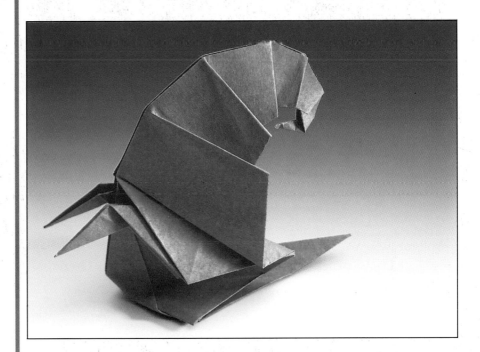

4. Combination fold, . . .

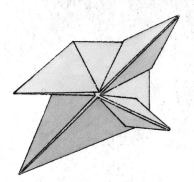

5. . . . pulling the corner outward; repeat steps 3 and 4 on the other side.

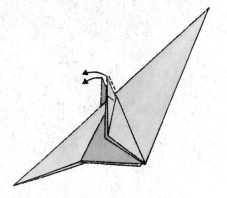

9. Push the point forward by combination folding to the inside.

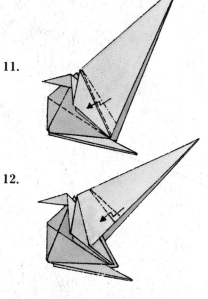

11.

12.

13.

11 to 13. Form the snail's shell with zigzag folds.

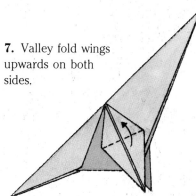

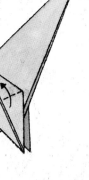

6. Mountain fold the figure together.

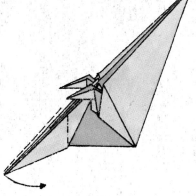

10. Fold left corner inward.

7. Valley fold wings upwards on both sides.

14. Valley fold upwards on both sides.

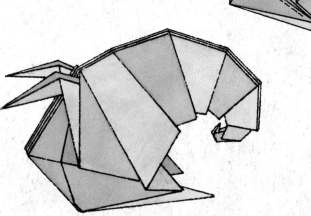

8. Fold wings together on both sides.

15. Completed snail.

Raven

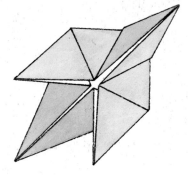

1. Starting point is step 3 of the Snail, based on Basic Form VI. Open up the lower part of the form.

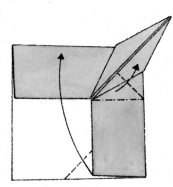

2. Pull upwards on the edge in the direction of the arrow and fold as marked.

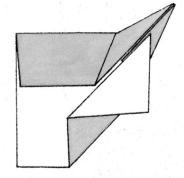

4. Repeat steps 2 and 3 on the other side.

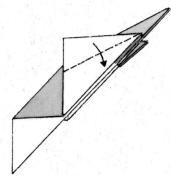

6. Valley fold on both sides.

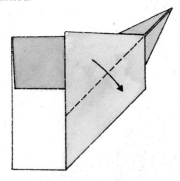

3. Valley fold to the right.

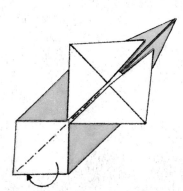

5. Fold the figure together in the middle.

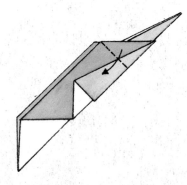

7. Bend corners downwards on both sides.

8. Valley fold to the right and . . .

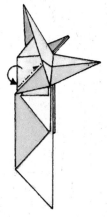

9. . . . mountain fold to the left, so that the head is pressed downwards.

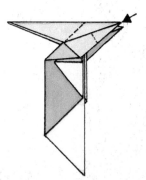

10. With a combination fold, place the corner marked onto the opposite corner.

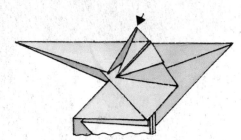

11. Bend the upper tip inward.

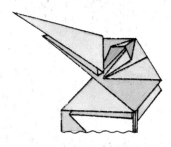

12. Repeat steps 10 and 11 on the reverse; with zigzag fold, . . .

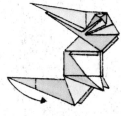

13. . . . form the head.

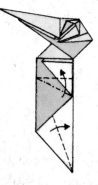

14. Combination fold upwards as marked and fold lower corner towards the outer edge.

15. Valley fold; repeat steps 14 and 15 on the reverse.

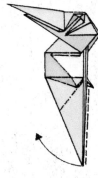

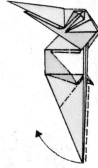

16. Combination fold, placing the lower point inside and to the left.

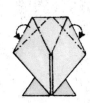

17. Fold the point inward.

18. Mountain fold the edges of the footing downwards.

19. Completed raven.

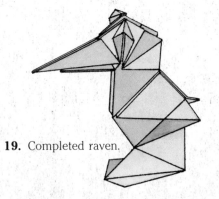

Rhinoceros

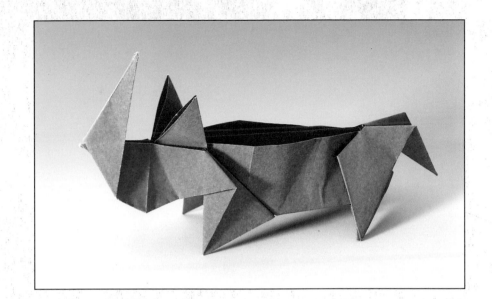

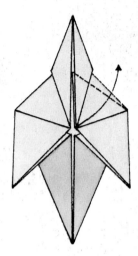

1. Starting point is step 3 of the Snail, based on Basic Form VI. Pull the corner upwards as marked, in the direction of the arrow, . . .

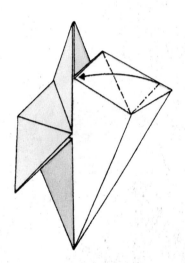

2. . . . and bend it towards the middle.

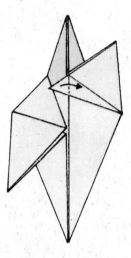

3. Fold the edge upwards as shown.

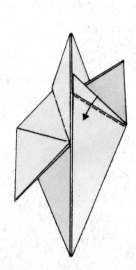

4. Valley fold downwards.

5. Fold point to the right; repeat steps 1 to 5 on the other side.

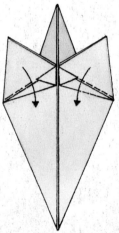

6. Fold wings downwards; place little corner flaps over them again.

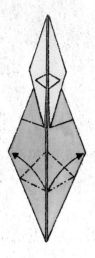

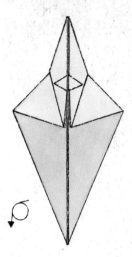

7. Turn over the form.

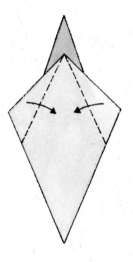

8. Valley fold inward.

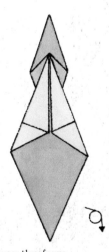

9. Turn over the form.

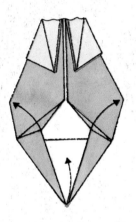

10. Open up the folding piece slightly, then combination fold, . . .

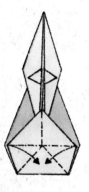

11. . . . and pull the lower corner upwards and fold it as shown (partial view).

12. With a combination fold, bend both corners . . .

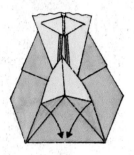

13. . . . downwards.

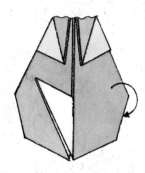

14. Fold entire figure together backwards up the middle.

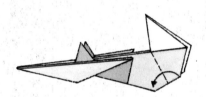

15. Valley fold on the front and . . .

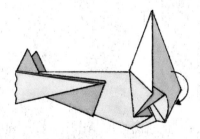

16. . . . on the back, so that the tail is pressed slightly downwards.

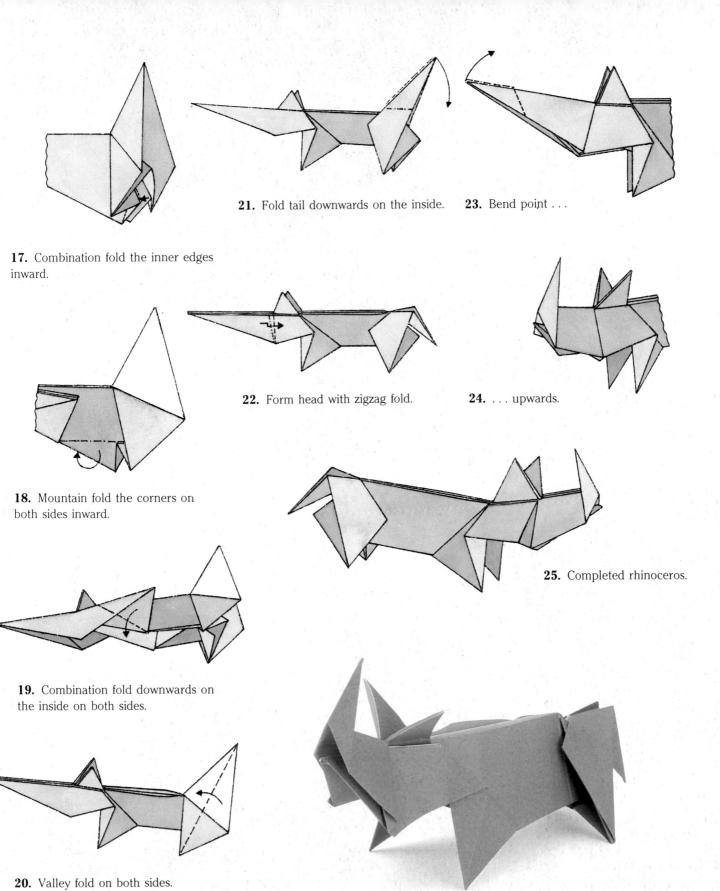

21. Fold tail downwards on the inside.

23. Bend point . . .

17. Combination fold the inner edges inward.

22. Form head with zigzag fold.

24. . . . upwards.

18. Mountain fold the corners on both sides inward.

25. Completed rhinoceros.

19. Combination fold downwards on the inside on both sides.

20. Valley fold on both sides.

Basic Form VII

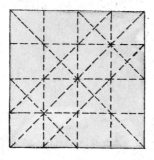

1. Prefold a square piece of paper at the marked lines.

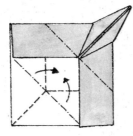

2. Turning the white side upwards, do Basic Form V folds steps 2 to 5. Valley fold as marked, . . .

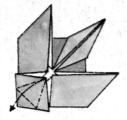

5. Combination fold; pulling the open corner of the square downwards and press.

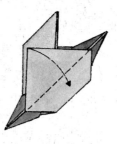

8. Valley fold at the middle line.

3. . . . so the point is turned upwards.

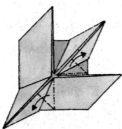

6. Open a side wing at the center point of the figure . . .

9. Repeat steps 6 to 8 on the other side.

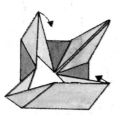

4. Press the outer edge of the corner downwards.

7. . . . and fold it to the opposite side.

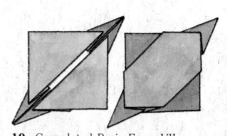

10. Completed Basic Form VII.

Horse

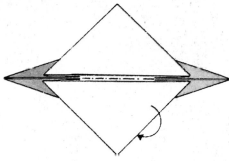

1. Starting point is Basic Form VII. Mountain fold the form in the middle.

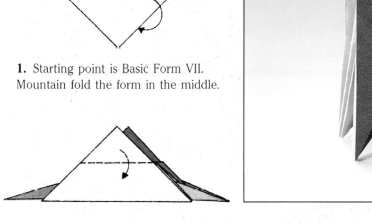

2. Valley fold downwards on both sides.

3. Valley fold to the left . . .

4. . . . and mountain fold on the reverse, so that the point is turned upwards.

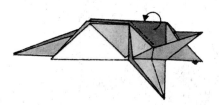

5. Repeat steps 3 and 4 on the other side.

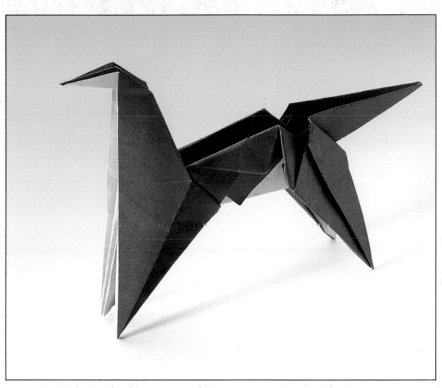

6. Mountain fold to the inside on the front and rear sides.

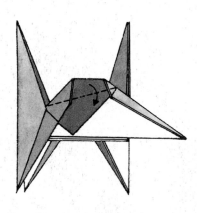

8. Valley fold downwards.

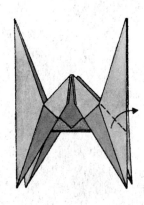

7. Fold outward, opening up surfaces.

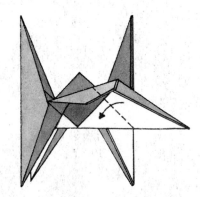

9. Fold surfaces inward again.

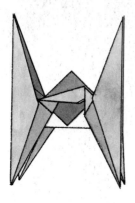

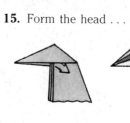

15. Form the head . . .

16. . . . as shown.

10. Repeat steps 7 to 9 on the reverse.

13. . . . to the outside again.

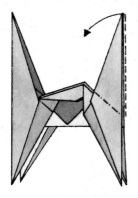

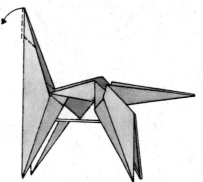

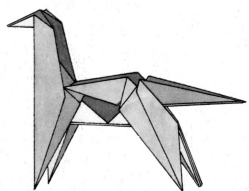

11. With a combination fold, bend the point . . .

14. Bend the point forward.

17. Completed horse.

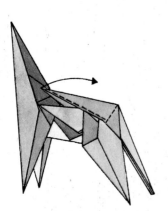

12. . . . inward, and fold where marked . . .

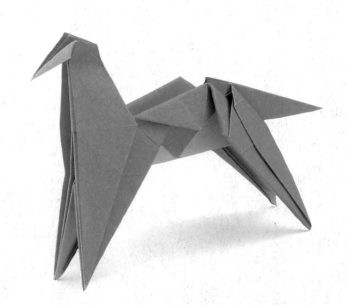

Cow

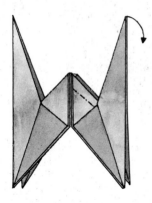

1. Starting point is step 5 of the Horse, based on Basic Form VII. Push the right side, as marked, . . .

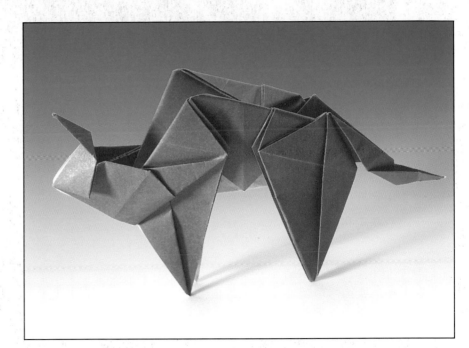

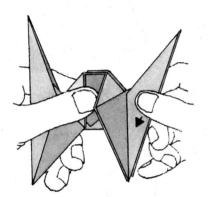

2. . . . upwards.

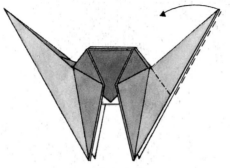

4. Combination fold the point inward . . .

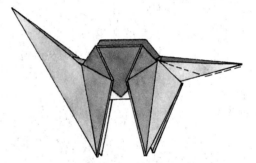

6. Combination fold downwards on the outside.

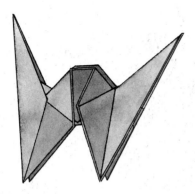

3. Repeat this step on the other side.

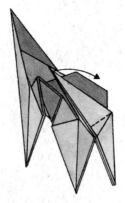

5. . . . and outward again as marked.

7. Bend the point upwards.

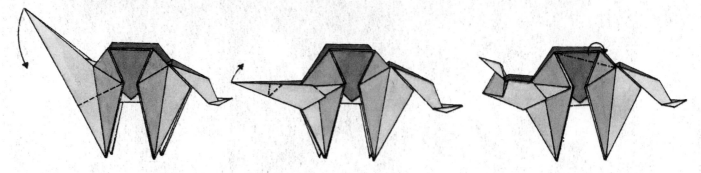

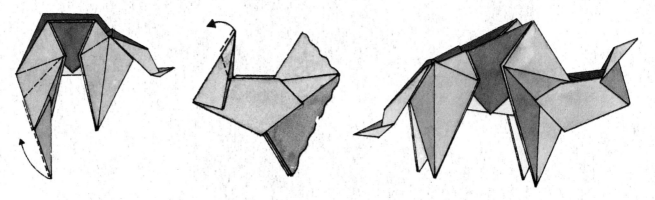

8. Fold the point downwards on the outside . . .

10. Form the head with a zigzag fold.

12. Mountain fold inward on both sides.

9. . . . and bend it upwards again as marked.

11. Bend the point forward.

13. Completed cow.

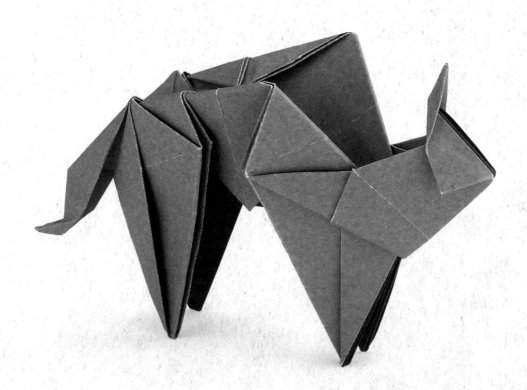

Camel

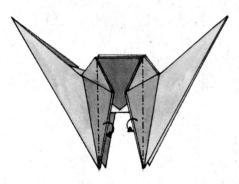

1. Starting point is step 3 of the Cow, based on Basic Form VII. Mountain fold to the inside at all four legs.

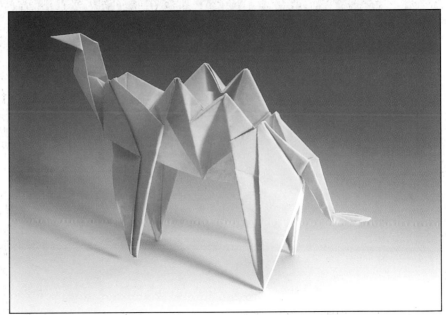

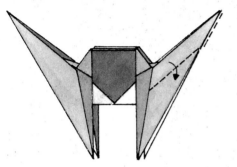

2. At the marking, bend the right point to the outside.

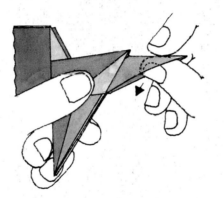

4. . . . and press it flat.

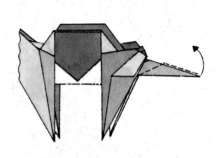

6. With a combination fold, bend the point upwards.

3. Pull point slightly downwards . . .

5. Press upper point inward.

7. Form the head.

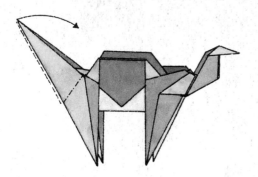

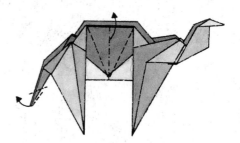

8. Press left point inward . . .

11. Make the sides of the point smaller.

13. Form tail point; combination fold as marked.

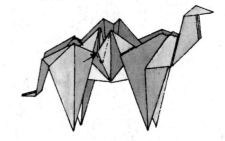

9. . . . and fold it outward again at the marking.

12. Bend the tail downwards.

14. Bend middle hump inward.

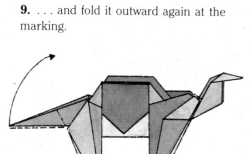

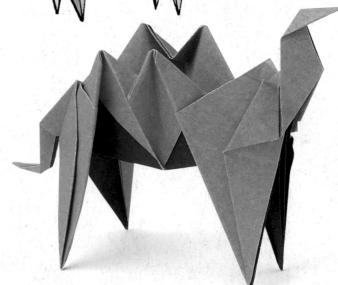

10. Bend the point upwards on the inside.

15. Completed camel.

Basic Form VIII

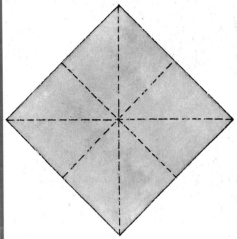

1. Prefold a square piece of paper at the marked lines.

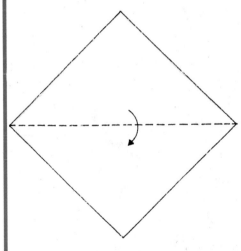

2. Turn the white side upwards and valley fold.

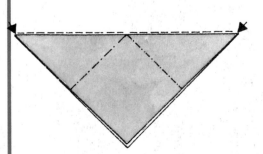

3. Fold the corners in on both sides.

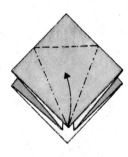

4. Pull the open corner of the square upwards . . .

5. . . . and fold it as shown.

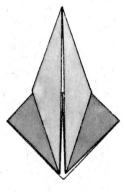

6. Repeat steps 4 and 5 on the reverse.

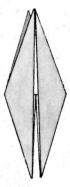

7. Completed Basic Form VIII; known as the "bird form."

Fish

1. Starting point is Basic Form VIII. Combination fold, standing the point vertically upwards.

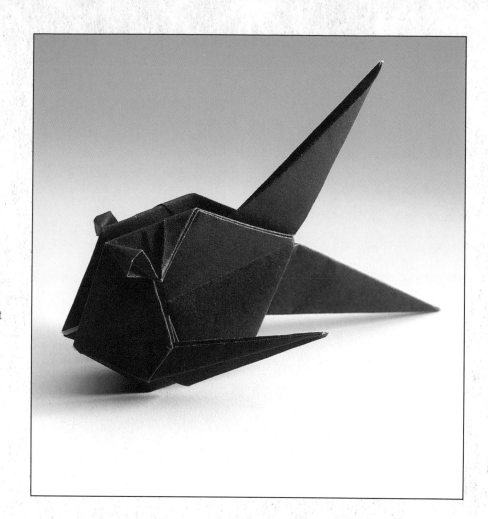

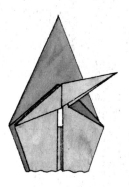

2. Repeat this step on the reverse. The valley folds run right along the edges of the triangle behind.

3. Fold the left front surface to the right, the right rear surface to the left.

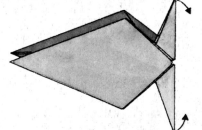

4. Pull both points . . .

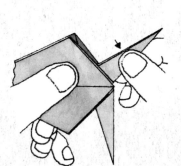

5. . . . slightly to the right.

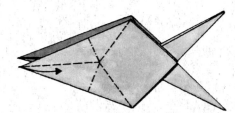

6. Combination fold so that the tip points vertically upwards.

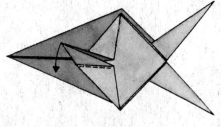

7. Bend the point downwards.

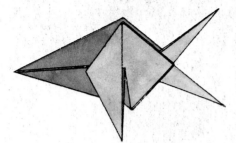

8. Repeat steps 6 and 7 on the reverse.

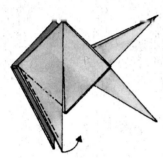

9. Turn the lower surfaces inward with a combination fold.

10. Bend the front section inward.

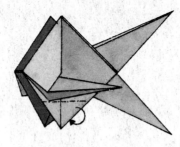

12. Bend the lower corner inward.

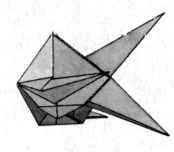

13. Repeat the step on the reverse.

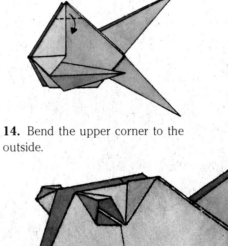

11. Repeat steps 9 and 10 on the reverse.

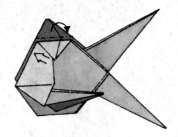

15. Pull outward the edge that lies underneath.

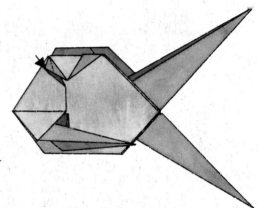

16. Form an eye; repeat steps 14 and 15 on the reverse.

14. Bend the upper corner to the outside.

17. Completed fish.

Bat

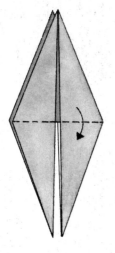

1. Starting point is Basic Form VIII. Open up the wings that point upwards.

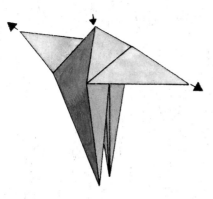

2. Pull the form carefully by the wings, to create a level area.

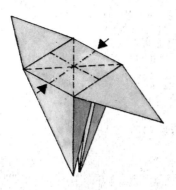

3. Press the form together, combination folding inward.

4. Fold the wings upwards again.

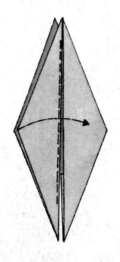

5. Fold the left front wing onto the right front wing, and the right rear wing onto the left rear wing.

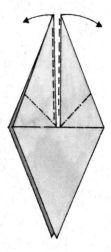

6. Combination fold downwards to the inside on both sides.

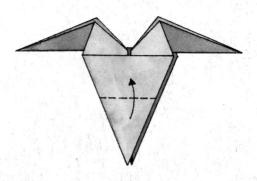

7. Valley fold upwards.

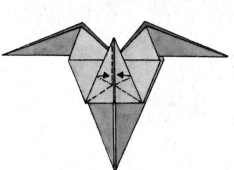

8. Combination fold, so that the tip stands upwards.

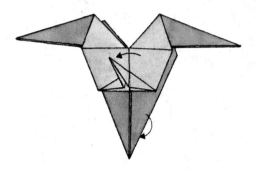

9. Fold front and back sides together.

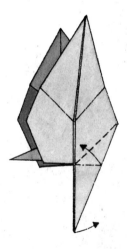

10. Combination fold upwards to the outside.

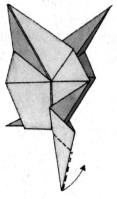

11. Bend the point downwards . . .

12. . . . and upwards again.

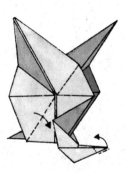

13. Bend the point tip upwards; valley fold both wings forward at the marking.

14. Form head with mountain fold . . .

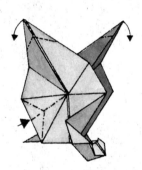

15. . . . inward, then pressing flat.

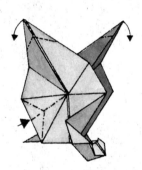

16. Form wings with combination folds.

17. Completed bat.

Owl

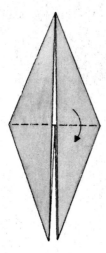

1. Starting point is Basic Form VIII. Fold the front upper section downwards.

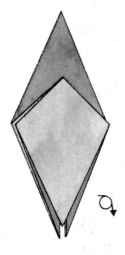

2. Turn over the folding piece, so that the three tips point upwards.

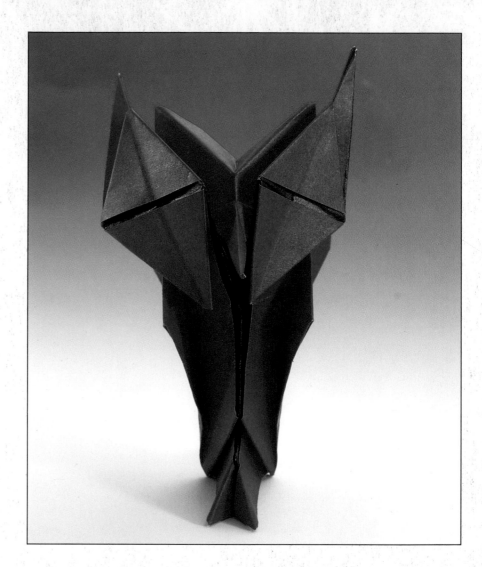

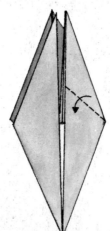

3. Place wing to stand up.

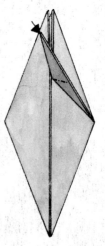

4. Push down on the tip of the wing with your finger to open, ...

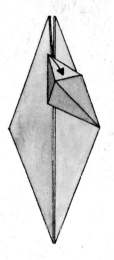

5. . . . then press the upper point to the outside.

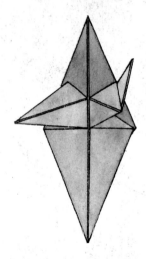

8. Combination fold so that the point stands up, . . .

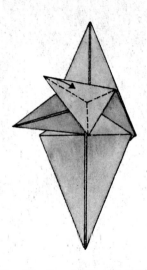

11. Repeat steps 7 to 10 on the left side.

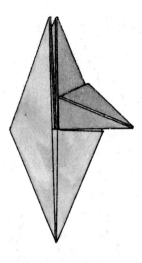

6. Repeat steps 3 to 5 on the other side.

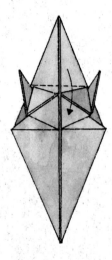

9. . . . then fold it upwards.

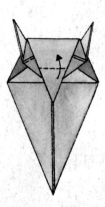

12. Bend upper point downwards.

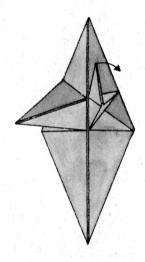

7. Valley fold upwards.

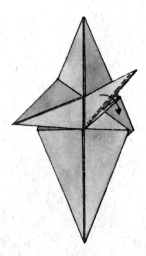

10. Unfold the top flap towards the right.

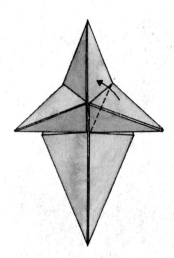

13. Valley fold upwards.

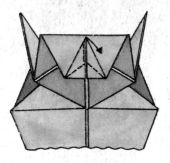

14. Combination fold the point to stand vertically.

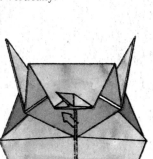

15. Cover the lower portion of the flap with the eye foldings, so that only the beak juts out.

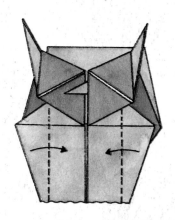

16. Valley fold to the inside.

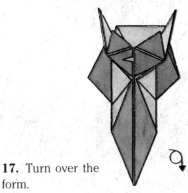

17. Turn over the form.

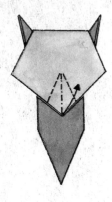

18. Pull point upwards.

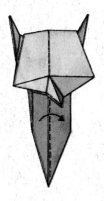

19. Fold entire figure in half towards the back.

20. Fold lower point upwards and to the inside, . . .

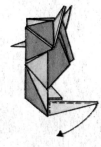

21. . . . then bend the point forward again as marked.

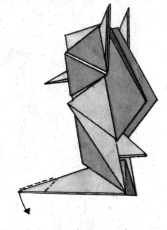

22. Bend the tip downwards . . .

23. . . . and fold it to the inside; then form beak and head.

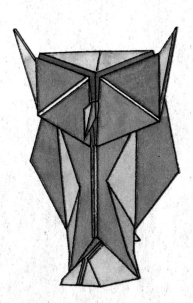

24. Completed owl.

Swan

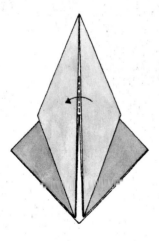

1. Starting point is step 6 of Basic Form VIII. Fold together the two front wings to the left, and the two rear wings to the right.

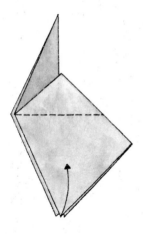

2. Fold the lower corner upwards and press down the edges of the created square.

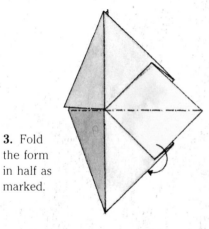

3. Fold the form in half as marked.

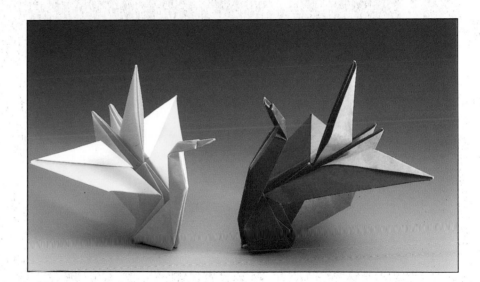

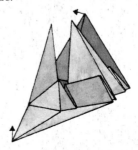

4. Open up the form.

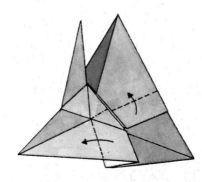

5. Valley fold each side upwards as marked . . .

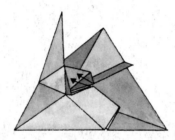

6. . . . and press the under surfaces together.

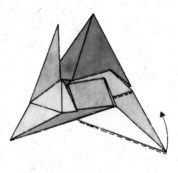

7. Combination fold upwards to the inside.

8. Fold form together in the middle.

9. Pull left middle point outward slightly and press it down.

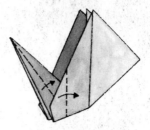

10. Valley fold at the marked lines.

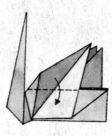

14. Valley fold downwards.

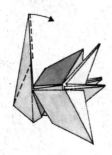

17. Fold the neck to the rear.

11. Repeat the step on the reverse.

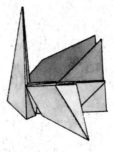

15. Repeat steps 12 to 14 on the reverse.

18. Bend the head forward again.

12. With combination fold, bend the right lower corner . . .

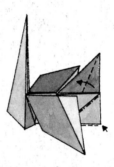

16. Combination fold the right lower corner on the front and back sides upwards and to the inside.

19. Form beak with zigzag fold.

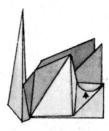

13. . . . up and to the inside.

20. Completed swan.

Basic Form IX

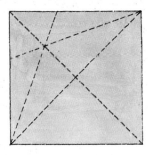

1. Prefold a square piece of paper at the marked lines.

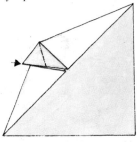

2. Valley fold, so that the point stands vertically upwards.

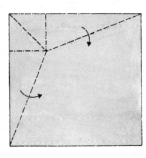

3. Press the tip to open, then push the outer edges down.

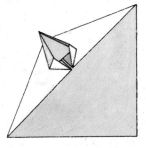

5. ... then pull the open corner upwards.

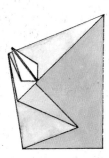

7. Repeat the step on the other side.

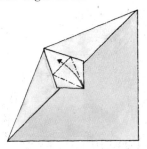

4. Combination fold; ...

6. Combination fold, placing the outer edge in position along the middle fold.

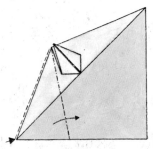

8. Completed Basic Form IX.

Crocodile

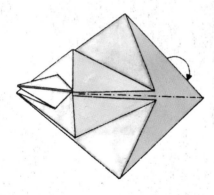

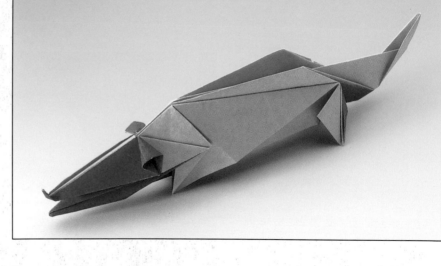

1. Starting point is Basic Form IX. Fold form together along the center line.

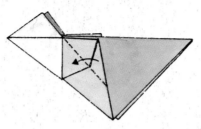

2. Valley fold upwards on both sides.

5. Turn corner down.

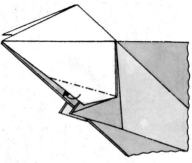

8. Mountain fold to the inside.

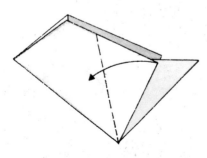

3. Valley fold forward on both sides as shown.

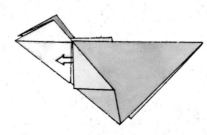

6. Open flap and move the corner below in and to the left.

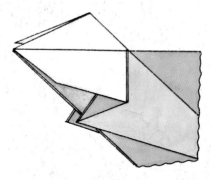

9. Repeat steps 5 and 8 on the reverse.

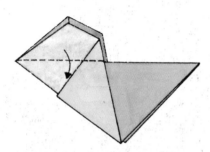

4. Valley fold downwards on both sides.

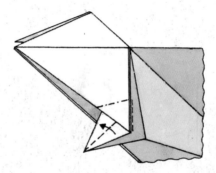

7. Combination fold to the inside.

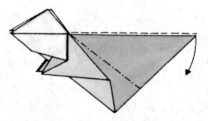

10. Combination fold downwards on the inside.

70

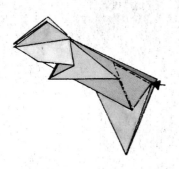

11. Combination fold again downwards on the inside.

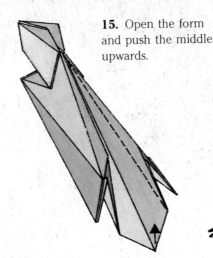

15. Open the form and push the middle upwards.

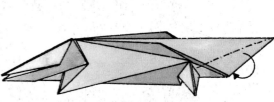

18. Repeat the step on the reverse.

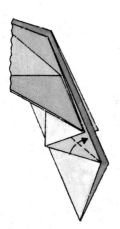

12. Repeat the step on the reverse.

16. Valley fold downwards on both sides.

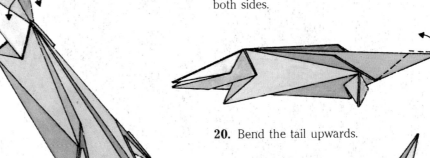

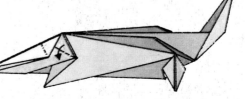

19. Mountain fold to the inside on both sides.

20. Bend the tail upwards.

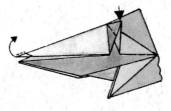

13. Bend corner upwards with combination fold.

21. Combination fold on both sides, so that the tail tip points upwards.

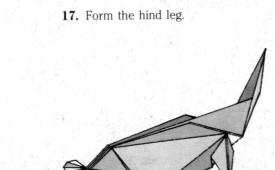

17. Form the hind leg.

14. Repeat the step on the reverse.

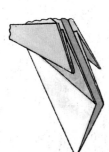

22. Form the eyes and mouth.

23. Completed crocodile.

Pigeon

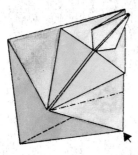

1. Starting point is Basic Form IX. Combination fold to the inside.

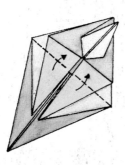

2. Repeat the step on the other side.

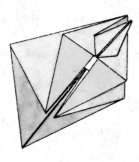

3. Fold the wing upwards.

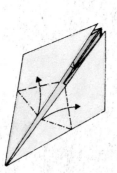

4. Combination fold upwards, . . .

5. . . . then pull the lower corner upwards and fold it as shown.

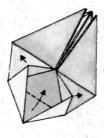

6. Combination fold, so that the tip is pointing upwards.

7. Fold the form together to the back.

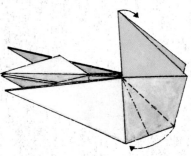

8. Push the tip and combination fold as marked . . .

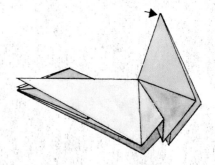

9. . . . to the inside on both sides.

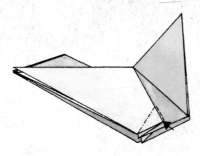

10. Combination fold the corner . . .

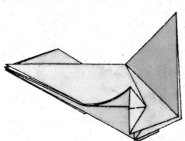

11. . . . to the inside; repeat the step on the reverse.

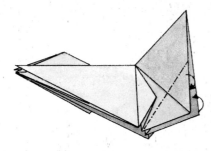

12. Fold the rear corners inward with mountain folds.

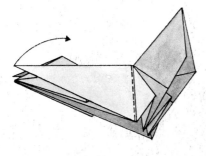

13. Valley fold both wings to the rear.

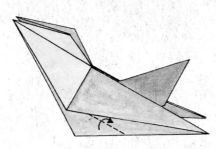

14. On the front and back, lift the upper wing and valley fold the surface beneath . . .

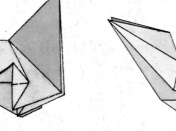

15. . . . upwards. Close up the figure again.

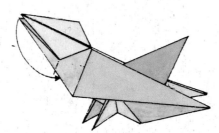

16. Fold the lower part of the point inward.

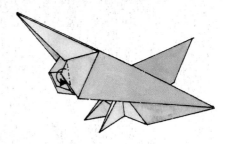

17. Fold the corners on both sides to the inside.

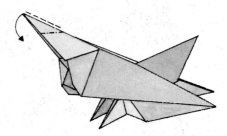

18. Bend the point inward and down for the head.

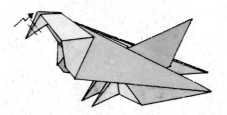

19. With a zigzag fold, form . . .

20. . . . the beak.

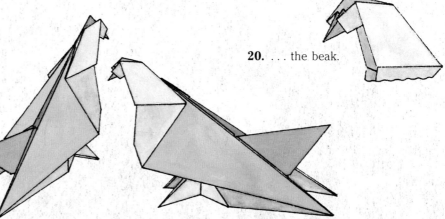

21. Completed pigeon.

Basic Form X

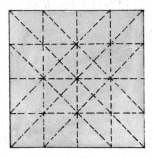

1. Prefold a square piece of paper as shown in the drawing.

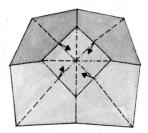

2. Mountain fold at the marked lines.

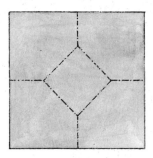

3. Push the paper together at the spots marked with arrows . . .

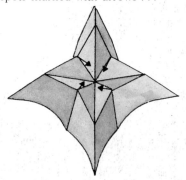

4. . . . all at the same time.

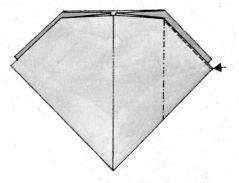

5. Combination fold to the inside.

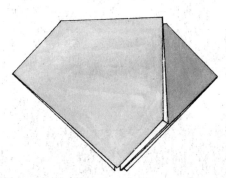

6. Repeat the fold at the other three corners.

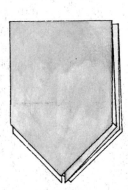

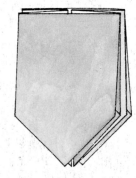

7. Completed Basic Form X.

Rose

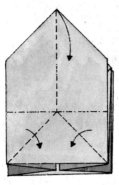

1. Starting point is Basic Form X. Press the front parts together and combination fold so that . . .

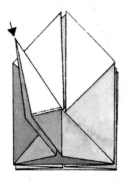

2. . . . the point stands upright. Push tip of point to open fold, and press square flat.

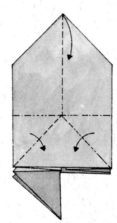

4. Repeat steps 1 and 2.

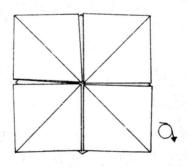

6. Turn over the form.

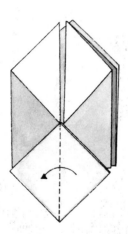

3. Fold the front right section to the left.

5. Work the other parts following steps 1 to 3; open up form.

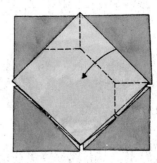

7. Valley fold to the middle point, so that both corners stand pointing upwards.

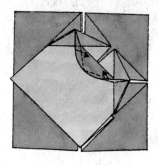

8. Fold corners to the middle point.

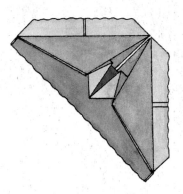

9. Repeat steps 7 and 8 on the remaining three sides.

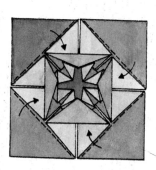

10. Fold the outer edges to the middle point.

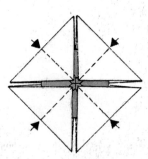

11. Push the paper together, valley folding at all lines as marked, at the same time.

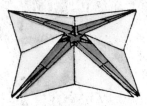

12. Turn over the form, so the middle is pointing downwards.

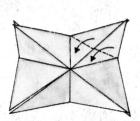

13. Bend the corners to the inside.

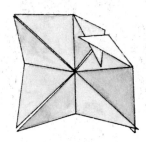

14. Place one corner inside . . .

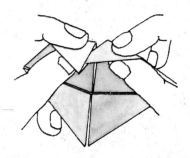

15. . . . the other corner.

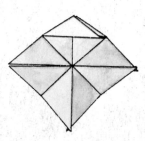

16. Repeat steps 13 to 15 on the remaining three sides.

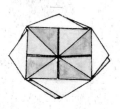

17. Turn over the form.

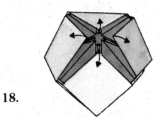

18.

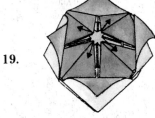

19.

20.

18 to 20. Slightly bend all petals towards the outside.

21. Completed rose.

Spider

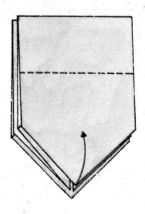

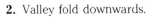

1. Starting point is Basic Form X. Valley fold upwards.

2. Valley fold downwards.

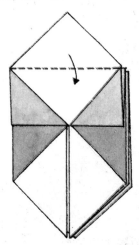

3. Fold front right section to the left.

4. Work the other sections following steps 1 to 3.

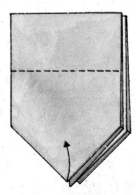

5. Combination fold the corner inward.

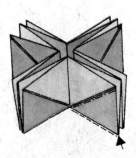

6.

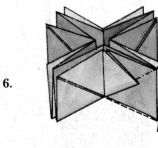

7.

6 and 7. Do the same at the remaining seven corners.

8. Fold the form together inward as marked.

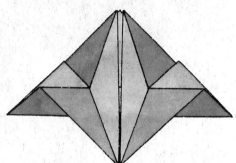

12. Repeat the step on the reverse.

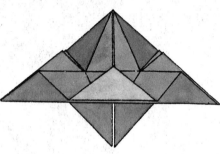

16. Repeat steps 14 and 15 on the reverse.

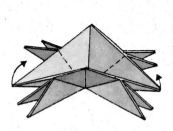

9. Combination fold the two marked points upwards, towards the middle.

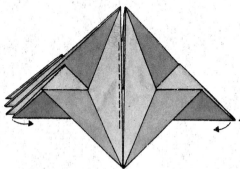

13. Fold together the two front parts upwards, and the two rear parts downwards.

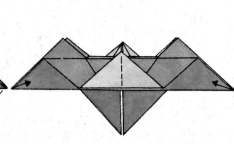

17. Fold together the two front parts upwards, and the two rear parts downwards.

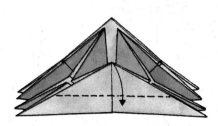

10. Combination fold, then pull the upper corner down and . . .

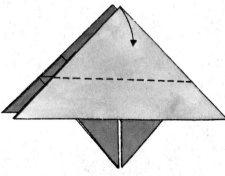

14. Valley fold downwards . . .

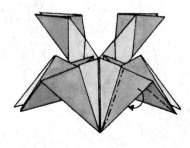

18. Turn the form around 90 degrees and tilt it slightly. Combination fold to the inside.

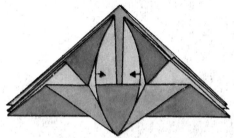

11. . . . fold the sides flat.

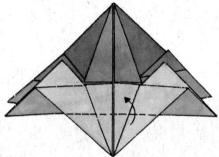

15. . . . and at the marking upwards again.

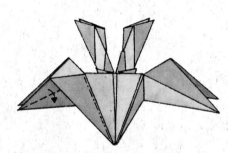

19. Repeat the step on the other side.

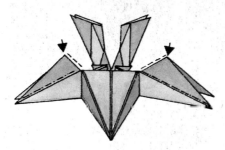

20. Combination fold downwards on the inside at the two front corners.

21. Mountain fold backwards . . .

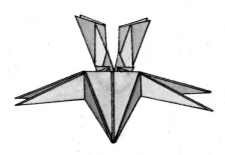

22. . . . the second rear pair of legs.

23. Press the tip pointing downwards up, so that . . .

24. . . . it is level with the leg pairs. Combination fold the marked corners upwards on the inside.

25. Push in to form the head.

26. Finish the head.

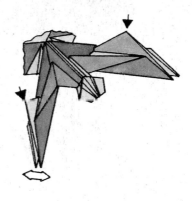

27. Open up each of the front leg forms and combination fold the marked corners . . .

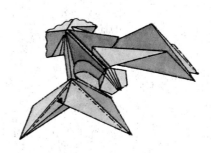

28. . . . inward and down.

29. Form the four front legs.

30. Completed spider.

Index